PUBLIC RELATIONS IN PRACTICE

Public Relations in Practice

Kate S. Kurtin

New York   Oxford
OXFORD UNIVERSITY PRESS

Oxford University Press is a department of the University of Oxford.
It furthers the University's objective of excellence in research, scholarship,
and education by publishing worldwide. Oxford is a registered trade mark of
Oxford University Press in the UK and certain other countries.

Published in the United States of America by Oxford University Press
198 Madison Avenue, New York, NY 10016, United States of America.

© 2019 by Oxford University Press

Library of Congress Cataloging-in-Publication Data

Names: Kurtin, Kate S., editor.
Title: Public relations in practice / edited by Kate S. Kurtin, PhD.
Description: New York : Oxford University Press, [2019]
Identifiers: LCCN 2018032420 (print) | LCCN 2018034835 (ebook)
   | ISBN 9780190912086 (ebook) | ISBN 9780190912079 (pbk.)
Subjects: LCSH: Public relations.
Classification: LCC HD59 (ebook) | LCC HD59 .P7953 2019 (print)
   | DDC 659.2—dc23
LC record available at https://lccn.loc.gov/2018032420

9 8 7 6 5 4 3 2 1
Printed by Sheridan Books, Inc., United States of America

Dedicated to D. Robert DeChaine,
my mentor, colleague, and friend.
You will always live on in the people
you left behind.

CONTENTS

Introduction   ix
Acknowledgments   xi

Chapter 1.   Corporate Public Relations by Steve Krizman   1

Chapter 2.   Consumer/Lifestyle Public Relations by Erik Perez   14

Chapter 3.   Internal Communications in Public Relations
             by Jasmine Myers   19

Chapter 4.   Health Communication in Public Relations
             by Christina Trinchero   31

Chapter 5.   Nonprofit Public Relations by Jillian Kanter   47

Chapter 6.   Community Relations and Public Relations
             by Jack Pflanz   59

Chapter 7.   Government Public Relations by Arlene Guzman   72

Chapter 8.   Public Affairs in Public Relations by Nicole
             Kuklok-Waldman   85

Chapter 9.   Crisis Management in Public Relations by Devon Nagle   95

Chapter 10. Event Planning and Public Relations by Gineen Cargo   105

Chapter 11. Branding in Public Relations by Jacqueline Camacho-Ruiz   114

Chapter 12. Public Relations Resources by Kate S. Kurtin   122

Greetings and welcome to *Public Relations in Practice*. My name is Dr. Kurtin and I am a professor of Communication at California State University, Los Angeles (Cal State LA). When I was hired at Cal State LA, over 80 percent of our students were public relations (PR) majors. The department brought me in to shake up the program and add an "applied element" to the classroom. I interpreted that as a directive to help our students get jobs, and I thought: What could be a better way to do that than to introduce students to people who already have the jobs they want?

While I am fortunate to live in Los Angeles, where I have easy access to many PR professionals, not all PR teachers are so lucky. Thus, the key goal for *Public Relations in Practice* is to bring practical experience into PR classrooms all over the world. This book strives to fill this need through a series of guest lecture chapters written by PR practitioners from all areas of the field (consumer products, branding, Fortune 500, health, nonprofit, etc.). These practitioners use each chapter to discuss their path, their experiences, what they wished they had known, specific case studies, and practical tips for getting into the industry. What started as a bit of a pipe dream has now become a reality.

Organization of the Book

Each chapter of *Public Relations in Practice* represents a guest lecture from an extremely qualified and talented member of the public relations community. Respectively, each chapter focuses on the guest lecturer's particular education, training, misunderstandings, common pitfalls, best practices, and will also walk the reader through how a trained professional thinks. Further, because I myself am a professor in the field, I understand the value in keeping the focus of the book on helping the reader make the transition from student to practitioner.

This book therefore serves as the connection between a more traditional scholarly textbook introducing abstract case studies and the personal and practical characteristics needed to succeed in the industry. In addition, this book strives to dispel one common misconception about PR: that it is all celebrity or brand management. In truth, the field is vast and diverse, but few students can ever be exposed to the true breadth of PR careers through a typical classroom experience. As a result, this book goes beyond any textbook in PR and opens the reader up to a vast array of options in the field of PR.

One final and important element of this book is its diverse representation. PR is a heterogeneous field and this book embodies that fact. In addition to diversity of age and experience, this text features narratives from practitioners of different races, ethnicities, educations, and geographical locations. The authors also talk about diversity in their careers—including their triumphs and hurdles. Lastly, each chapter features the author's headshot, so the reader can put a face to each name, hopefully helping the reader identify with the narrative and increase self-efficacy.

Pedagogical Features

Each chapter in *Public Relations in Practice* hosts an important set of features and tools. These include background on the author, case studies, tactics, and tips for success. In addition, each chapter addresses foundations, strategy, tactics, and contexts of public relations based on the author's own experiences and in the author's own words. As a result, these guest lectures put public relations into a practical, real-world context by presenting the narratives of practitioners in the field. It is an attempt to take the classroom from a passive mindset to a more active experience for students. This book allows access when it is not feasible to invite practitioners to visit in person.

About the Editor

Kate S. Kurtin, PhD, is an Assistant Professor of Communication Studies at California State University, Los Angeles. She received her undergraduate degree from Occidental College after studying sociology with a particular interest in media effects. She continued her education at Boston University where she received her MA for her work in advertising and communication research. Following this, she worked as an account planner in a few advertising agencies in the Boston area, and then spent two years as a market researcher before leaving the business world to go back to school one more time. Delving deeper into the role of advertising and media in the lives of children, she received her PhD in mass communication from the University of Connecticut.

With her background in advertising and media effects, Dr. Kurtin came to Cal State LA in 2013 to work on strategic and applied communication. Her continuing passion within communication studies is the media's effect on children, and, to that end, Dr. Kurtin studies the evolving way that young people use media within this frame.

Dr. Kurtin is the faculty advisor for The Cal State LA PRSSA chapter, as well as the Communication Studies Department student run marketing agency, ZenX-LA.

Acknowledgments

The main ideas of this book and how cool it would be came over drinks in a tiny Starbucks in Los Angeles with Arlene Guzman. At the time, we were writing a chapter for *Cases in Public Relations Strategy* (edited by St. John, Martinelli, Pritchard, and Spaulding, 2018) and talking about the changes happening within PR instruction at Cal State LA. Thank you, Arlene, for that, and for the many brainstorming sessions that followed. This book would not have happened without you. Thank you also to my incredible communication colleagues at Cal State LA. I am grateful every day for your support, guidance, and friendship. Starting from my first semester, Beryl Bellman has been telling me to "just write a book." Well Beryl, I finally did it! Thank you to the reviewers of this manuscript, Priya Lothe Doshi, Amy Hitt, Pamela D. Schultz, Jennifer F. Wood, and those who chose to remain anonymous, for providing helpful feedback. Thank you also to the talented authors: Gineen Cargo, Jacqueline Camacho-Ruiz, Arlene Guzman, Jillian Kanter, Steve Krizman, Nicole Kuklok-Waldman, Jasmine Myers, Devon Nagle, Erik Perez, Jack Pflanz, and Christina Trinchero, whose personality, experience, and dedication will help train the next generations of PR professionals. Thank you to my family, Andrew, Luke, and Griffin, who allowed PR to dominate the dinner conversation, and who now know more about public relations than any other people at the playground. You are the reasons why I work so hard. Finally, thank you to OUP for seeing the potential in this project and making our vision a reality.

1 CORPORATE PUBLIC RELATIONS

Steve Krizman

 Steve Krizman is a marketing and PR change agent who has led innovation in healthcare, journalism, and higher education. He currently is serving as interim associate vice president of marketing and communications at Metropolitan State University of Denver, and also is a tenure-track professor of PR and journalism at the university. In addition to that, he is an executive consultant for Healthcare for Intelligent Demand, a marketing strategy agency with a growing healthcare client base.

Part I: Personal

I am one lucky guy. I get paid to write.

That's exactly what I set out to do when I earned my bachelor's degree in journalism. I saw myself covering cops and courts, going to disaster scenes, interviewing the mighty, and pumping out articles that educated and entertained. I saw myself working up from the small dailies until I was an editor at a big-city newspaper.

And I did that, becoming assistant city editor at the *Rocky Mountain News* in Denver in the 1990s. But having reached my journalistic goal, I was not happy. I felt trapped in telling the same old shallow stories of scandal and weather.

So, I did what I had sworn I never would do: I jumped over to public relations—the dark side, as we journalists called it.

Following My Values

But I chose to do media relations for a corporate organization I could believe in: Kaiser Permanente, a nonprofit that provided health insurance and healthcare. At a time when insurance companies and hospitals were turning into for-profit behemoths, Kaiser Permanente was a throwback. It was founded in the 1940s by Dr. Sidney Garfield and industrialist Henry Kaiser to ensure quality healthcare for the people building the California Aqueduct in the southern California desert. The workers set aside a few pennies from each paycheck to fund a medical clinic that provided all their care and their families' care at no additional cost.

It's more complicated than that now, but the Kaiser Permanente soul is in the idea that everyone deserves good healthcare, and that it can be provided most effectively and affordably when the medical team works together for the benefit of the patient (as opposed to the benefit of investors).

My On-the-Job Training

I joined Kaiser Permanente's Colorado Region as its media relations representative and editor of its member magazine in 1999. I felt like I was stepping into the abyss: I had never taken a media relations course and didn't know how to do it.

But it turns out that my experience as a reporter and editor made me perfect for media relations—the PR function that helps an organization tell its story and protect its reputation in print, broadcast, and online media. I knew how newsrooms work. I knew what interests reporters and what their work day is like. I could pitch story ideas to them that would be interesting to their readers *and* helpful to Kaiser Permanente.

As a journalist in a healthcare organization, my natural curiosity drew me into the operating rooms, exam rooms, and laboratories to find out how the medical world works. My years of showing up on the scene to interview strangers made it easy to talk to the doctors, nurses, physical therapists, and lab scientists. Daily news writing had taught me ways to describe complex concepts so they could more easily be understood: using an automotive metaphor, for example, to describe the filtering action of the human liver.

Every day, reporters and editors sift through hundreds of story ideas, choosing the few that they believed would interest their readers. This experience helped me to spot the trending stories that reporters and editors will want to localize, and the things to say that will make them want to interview the experts in my organization.

Corporate Communication Is More Than Media Relations

In large corporate organizations, the workers get so caught up in talking amongst themselves that they forget everyone and everything outside their walls—including their customers. The leadership and rank-and-file get so caught up in the *how* of doing things that they sometimes forget *why* they exist.

This is where the heavy, important, and often underrated work of internal and customer communication comes in. I used every trick I learned as a former journalist in my corporate communication role. I assembled teams of people whose varied communication talents were also important to this work—people with PR agency experience, video producers, website designers, social media community managers, artists, and people who were expert at plotting out the steps of a project and keeping everyone else on track.

I discovered that we communicators underestimate our superpowers. Not everyone can get outside themselves enough to discover and relate another's worries or desires. Not everyone can turn around and tell that person's story for them. Not everyone is tuned into the community psyche enough to know what resonates. Not everyone has the ability to clearly explain complex ideas.

Internal Communication: The Toughest Nut to Crack

My media relations duties quickly expanded to include internal communication. Primarily this was defined as helping the organization's leaders explain their plans to staff and physicians. Our nurses, therapists, and customer service representatives were represented by a union. Those groups are traditionally at each other's throats. In my role as internal communication adviser, I helped facilitate thorny discussions about things such as new technology that would disrupt workers' daily routines.

When human resources needed to announce changes in benefits, my team was called in to help. We developed articles for the employee newsletter, provided talking points to help managers explain the changes, and facilitated employee training sessions.

Those of us who have done any communication to influence know that it requires two-way channels so that the leaders can hear questions and comments from the front lines and respond in ways to help achieve understanding. Leaders, however, tend to think that all they have to do is say something and it will be understood and accepted across the organization. I learned valuable principles about internal communication from the book *Communicating for Managerial Effectiveness* by Phillip G. Clampitt.

I applied Clampitt's principles to the traditional model of communication to influence: that the audience starts with cluelessness and moves to awareness, and from there to understanding, commitment, and advocacy. Clampitt's "lean" communication tools are best for the early phases of that arc. Because they are one-way, lean communication tactics can raise awareness, but not much more. As we move up the arc toward understanding, we necessarily need to use more rich communication tools, because the audience has questions or pushback that needs to be addressed by the communicator. Then, to get someone to buy into your idea—to commit themselves to changing a behavior or an opinion—you need even richer tools, tools that will answer last-minute objections and make it easy to take the next step.

For example, the Colorado region of Kaiser Permanente was the first to implement an electronic medical record system. Computers would be installed in every exam room, clinicians would need to learn how to operate them, and patients would need to feel confident in their security and excited about the prospect of being able to access their medical record online.

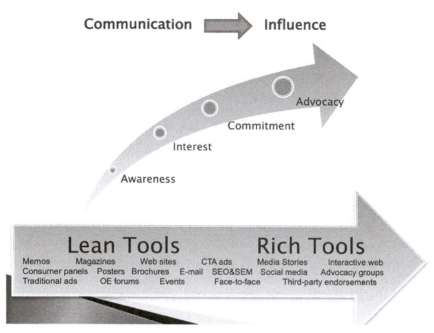

FIGURE 1.1 Model of Communication to Influence created by Steven Krizman.

To move our internal audience *from cluelessness to awareness*, we started with announcements in all channels: items in the weekly employee newsletter, blast emails, and posters in employee break rooms.

To ladder them up *from awareness to understanding*, we provided more information to management and labor leaders, who then would talk about the big change in staff meetings and one-on-one sessions.

Building commitment to the idea was a big leap. We were suggesting a major change in the way people did their work. Because of this shift, we also needed to help them see how it was going to make their jobs better and the patients happier. One component we implemented was to have top leaders in the organization, such as the chief medical officer, walk around the medical offices to answer questions from the doctors and nurses. Next, project leaders brought computers into the work areas to demonstrate. From these demonstrations and impromptu Q&A sessions, input from the front lines was incorporated into the design of the technology and the exam room workstations. Training procedures were mapped out, with staff and physicians having a say in timing and method of training.

Because of our solid, two-way communication, we had early adopters and a significant number of middle-of-the roaders ready to make the leap. Out of a dozen medical offices, two stepped up to be the first to implement. The new system was installed in those offices and communication team members were there to capture their stories.

Finally, our communication program *identified advocates* for this new way of doing things and encouraged them to help us bring others into commitment. We celebrated successful implementations, calling out individuals whose efforts we knew would be admired and emulated by others across the region. We had them stand up and take a bow at regional meetings. We hosted conference calls in which they talked with the other medical office leaders who were about to implement the system. These advocates helped their peers see ways to make this drastic change without too much pain and helped them envision the advantages that were on the other side of implementation.

Customer Communication: A Tough Nut, But More Fun

As we will see in the case study section of this chapter, a corporate communication team that integrates its work with marketing and advertising has a clear impact on the growth of the organization. A top concern of corporate communication is ensuring that customers are happy with having chosen you. If this is true, then they are more likely to choose you again *and* tell others that you are the right choice.

Over the last two decades, the country has wrestled with how to fairly and efficiently provide healthcare. I believed Kaiser Permanente had a solution. I joined a national group of Kaiser Permanente communicators who searched for ways to better tell our story and to overcome the negative stories that had built up over the years. In the course of this work, I learned the principles of branding. The core principle behind this is that a brand—the public's perception of an organization—is created and maintained by the public. Everything an organization does, says, and signals—good and bad—contributes to that public brand perception. An organization can influence the public perception by how it conducts itself. It cannot force a brand perception on the public.

Storytelling Is Key

I knew from experience and from the research that storytelling is the most influential form of communication. After helping the national program develop a groundbreaking branding initiative—known by its Thrive advertising campaign—I sought to use storytelling to nurture our image and reputation in the Colorado region.

In the early 2000s, upheaval in the media marketplace was changing the playing field for both public relations and advertising. It wasn't enough for either team to rely solely on established media to tell our story. Consumers were getting their information from many sources other than the traditional media outlets. PR could not get the job done simply by pitching stories to newspaper and TV reporters. Advertising could not cover all the potential customers by buying spots in traditional media.

Because of this change in the media landscape and in consumer's relationship with the media, Kaiser Permanente's PR, marketing, and advertising departments had a common problem and, I believed, a common tool: the organization's story. At our essence, each department was trying to get the best version of Kaiser Permanente's story to the right people at the right time in order to influence their thinking. Why not join forces?

I therefore proposed (and eventually became director of) the Integrated Communication and Brand Management department in Kaiser Permanente's Colorado region. This new department was responsible for internal and external communication, including marketing and advertising. The team was made up of former journalists, print and web designers, photographers, videographers, advertising copywriters, and marketing strategists.

This put all the players together on one team. More importantly, it put all the budget into one pot, to be strategically divided among all the potential channels available to us.

Now, then. How to do that?

Part II: Case Study on Preparing for the Affordable Care Act

In 2010, Congress passed the Affordable Care Act (ACA), which required health insurance companies to provide insurance to everyone who came to their door. Insurance companies previously could choose their customers and set their premiums based on patients' medical history. This antiquated system left 16 percent of the population without health insurance, which endangered their health and put the burden of covering their emergency care on the taxpayers.

Before the ACA, insurance companies remained in business by spreading the cost of healthcare across their customers. The big bills racked up by sick people were covered by the premiums paid by healthy people. In return, the healthy people expected their bills to be paid if and when they get sick.

The ACA's requirement that insurance companies cover everyone could have led to disaster. Healthy people could stay out of the insurance market until they got sick, then knock on the door for coverage and the company would be required to provide it, even though they had not paid into the kitty for all the years they were healthy.

To make this work, Congress made health insurance coverage a requirement for everyone. If you didn't get health insurance, you would be fined. This would ensure enough healthy people in the coverage pool to cover the cost of the sick. The ACA also established health insurance exchanges where consumers would compare the costs and benefits of different plans.

Main Objectives

The job of corporate communication was to coordinate information flow across many different departments, help make the workforce aware of the important ACA developments and what it meant to them, and use print, broadcast, and digital media as a conduit to the public. Because we were integrated with the marketing and advertising functions, the corporate communicators also shared the objective of reaching potential customers and encouraging them to choose Kaiser Permanente over our competitors.

Our goal was succinctly stated as: "win the exchange." We wanted the shoppers in the ACA insurance exchange in Colorado to choose us more frequently than any of our competitors. The objectives to achieve this:

1. Establish recognition of the Kaiser Permanente value proposition among people who would be buying through the new exchange so that we were on their consideration list when the exchanges opened in fall 2013.
2. Establish new channels to help individuals research and select Kaiser Permanente.
3. Ensure the staff and physicians were up to date on Kaiser Permanente's preparations for the exchange.
4. Position Kaiser Permanente as a leader in helping Coloradans obtain affordable, quality healthcare.

Timeline, Budget, and Technical Requirements

The ACA was signed into law in March 2010. The exchanges were required to be operational by October 2013. The state of Colorado started the process of establishing an exchange in the summer of 2011. We had to begin describing our plans to prospective purchasers in summer 2013.

Kaiser Permanente set aside a fund for extraordinary expenses that would be incurred during the preparation for entering the exchanges. But my integrated communication team was asked to reallocate its existing budget to cover added activities. We were able to seek additional funds on a case-by-case basis.

Ethical Considerations

There were two prime ethical considerations:

1. Do not choose sides in the political battle that was raging around ACA.
2. Fulfill our mission to provide quality healthcare to the underserved.

From the moment it was passed, congressional attempts were made to overturn the ACA. Partisan balance in Congress changed during the course of implementation, keeping the political debate on the front burner. Kaiser Permanente, as a nonprofit healthcare organization, could not and did not take a partisan position. Our official line was that we favored expanded, affordable coverage for all. We took no official positions on measures in Washington.

The staff and physicians of Kaiser Permanente, however, were generally in favor of the ACA. The communication team had to remain nonpartisan and help ensure that our workforce understood the importance of us remaining nonpartisan in the ongoing debate. It was important that we modeled a middle-of-the-road approach to implementing whatever program Washington came up with.

The second aspect of our ethical concern—fulfilling our mission to care for the underserved—impacted our strategy and our communication. For-profit insurance companies that did not have our ethical compass looked at the new healthcare exchanges as an opportunity to make money. The goal, for them, was to attract as many healthy people and as few sick people as possible. They tended to develop plans with hip names in a bid for the "young healthies."

The majority of the people who would gain insurance under the ACA were not young healthies, though. They were people whose employers did not provide insurance or did not cover family members. They were people who lost insurance because they had illnesses. Many had neglected to care for chronic illnesses, such as diabetes and heart disease, and would require a lot of initial care.

Kaiser Permanente's strategic decision was to create fair plans that would attract people of all circumstances. This led to a communication program that included events that attracted people of all socioeconomic backgrounds, and this included outreach to Spanish-language media.

Our Solution

We believed the challenge was uniquely suited to our strength as an integrated communication and marketing team. But we were still early in our integration, and this challenge would test our department to our limits. We committed ourselves to these principles:

1. **Our prime product was stories, and each story had to work hard.** Internal communicators told stories about what was happening in the organization. Media relations people were telling stories of interest to the public. Advertising and marketing teams were telling stories that touted the benefits of our insurance and care. Going forward, we had to make sure our stories were coordinated.
2. **Be evidence-based.** Communicating to influence opinions and behaviors is not an exact science. But it isn't a crapshoot, either: especially now that so much of our communication happens on digital platforms, there are ways to monitor the impact our words and visuals are having. We vowed to pay attention to the audience reactions and continually adjust our strategies, tactics, and messages accordingly.
3. **Be audience-centered.** There was no shortage of information to be shared. Our job was to make sure the right information got to the right people at

the right time. Corporate communicators, by virtue of our involvement across the organization, are in a unique position to understand the information needs and relevant messages for various audiences.

4. **Be curious, not furious.** The rules of the game would change. The organization's priorities would shift. Stress would build. When we felt frustration or anger bubbling, we tried to ask questions first.

Process Is Important

With so many moving parts needing coordination, the first order of business was to establish a process. An individual from each integrated communication discipline was designated to be the point person on all things related to the ACA. And within that group, one individual was designated as the quarterback. It was that person's role to be informed about all aspects of the team's work and to be the team expert on the ACA and Kaiser Permanente's response.

I was fortunate to have a former newspaper editor on the team. Luke Clarke and I had worked together at the *Rocky Mountain News*. He had years of experience juggling numerous issues and directing several people who were working on different projects. He was also an expert at taking complex information and converting it into clear language.

Anyone who has excellent communication skills *and* is good at planning and executing on a plan is worth their weight in gold on today's corporate communication team. More and more, communication team members are getting formal training in project management—there's a project management professional (PMP) certificate that can be earned, attesting to the mastering of the specific skills needed to get project plans down on paper and then using them to guide teams toward their goals.

Communication to Influence Model Applied

We listed our target audiences and then applied the communication to influence model (as shown in Fig. 1.1):

- **Staff and physicians:** What would it take to make them *aware* of the ACA issues (as they continually changed), help them *understand* what they needed to understand from their spot in the organization and get them to *commit* to the action needed to move us toward readiness?
- **Customers and patients:** What did they need to know today, tomorrow, and the day of ACA implementation? What questions would we need to answer to bring them to understanding? What actions would they need to take as the ACA went into effect?
- **Prospective customers:** How do we make them aware that Kaiser Permanente soon will be available to them? What concerns can we alleviate so they

can understand the value of health insurance in general and Kaiser Permanente in particular? How can we make it easy for them to commit to Kaiser Permanente when the time came for them to choose a health plan on the exchange?

- **Media and other external influencers, such as pundits and bloggers:** We needed to ensure they were aware of Kaiser Permanente's nonpartisan position *and* our commitment to meeting the challenge of a quick ACA implementation. We wanted them to commit to writing stories that were accurate and helpful to a confused public.

Research the Audiences

We researched our audiences' existing knowledge gaps:

- For staff and physicians, the ACA communication team met weekly and compared notes of what they had heard in meetings and what questions were coming into the internal communication team.
- For our customers and patients, we tapped into the customer call center and the frontline caregivers, finding out the questions and concerns they were hearing.
- For our prospective customers, we monitored research being conducted by national groups and we conducted our own ethnographic research. We gathered a sampling of uninsured people for group discussions and we met with them in their homes. This gave us a better understanding of the life issues that influence attitudes toward healthcare and health insurance.
- For media influencers, we tuned our media monitoring programs to the ACA frequency. We listened carefully for what topics and viewpoints were trending so that we could fashion our outward messages so that they fit into the conversation.

Strategic Storytelling

We began to engage in what is called "brand journalism" when it is practiced on the PR side of the house, and "content marketing" when it is practiced on the marketing side of the house.

In successful brand journalism and content marketing, you identify the key messages the organization needs to convey to its target audiences and you match those against the problems your key audiences are trying to solve. The stories you choose are the ones that satisfy both criteria.

For example, we identified a segment of potential buyers on the ACA exchange who once had coverage but lost it because they changed employers. We knew that their problem to solve was making a smart choice. We shared stories about Kaiser Permanente patients who had weighed their options and who believed they had made the right choice. We provided glossaries, FAQs, and other consumer-friendly, unbiased information.

In brand journalism, you aren't always extolling the virtues of your product or service. Often you are simply being helpful, expecting that you will thus be remembered when the consumer starts narrowing down options.

Measure the Right Things

Which brings us to evidence-based communication. Never have we enjoyed the visibility into our audiences' communication habits as we do today. But it's difficult to make sense of all the data available to us.

Starting with the research phase, we had access to this data:

- **Online healthcare shopping behaviors.** We could see the questions consumers were asking (Google search words). We could follow shoppers who visited our website and marketing landing pages to see what interested them (Google Analytics website statistics).
- **News and pundit trends.** We could capture the names and contact information for reporters and bloggers who were highly regarded by the public (Twitter and media tracking services such as Cision and Meltwater). We could identify key trends in the discussion (news aggregators such as Feedly).
- **Persona characteristics.** The data trail left by consumers as they go about their daily lives—shopping at the grocery store, selecting Netflix movies, buying on Amazon—is compiled by services such as Experian to create consumer archetypes that make it easier to target tightly defined demographics and psychographics down to the zip code.

As we executed our multifaceted communication and marketing campaign, we had access to data about:

- **Our fans.** We could monitor their support by way of their comments and shares of our Facebook and Twitter posts.
- **Potential customers' interest level.** When they visited our online shopping site, we could identify what content helped or hindered their shopping experience. Cookies placed in their browser allowed us to identify how they learned about us and where they went after they left our site.
- **Our staff and physicians' questions and concerns.** We monitored email open rates to see what percentage of our coworkers were accessing information we pushed out. We analyzed our intranet visits and referrals to see what content was most popular. We gathered and read comments on our stories to determine what needed more explanation or emphasis.

Were We Successful?

We won the Colorado exchange! Kaiser Permanente captured the largest share of consumers in the exchange: 31 percent, which was more than double our goal.

But claiming credit for success is tricky. There is much debate about how you measure attribution, crediting communication, and marketing activities for consumer actions. Our systems enabled us to measure how many people responded to an online advertisement and came to our shopping site, but we could not determine who among those leads went on to purchase our insurance on the state exchange. And how many of our new members were exposed to several different types of communication activities and which of those were most impactful?

The fact is, our health plans were the lowest priced. That undoubtedly had a significant impact on why we won the Colorado exchange. But how many people would *not* have known about our offering and our price if not for our PR and marketing outreach?

You can drive yourself crazy trying to draw connections between communication activities and ultimate sales. The better option is to measure:

1. Actions directly impacted by the communication intervention, and
2. The subset of those actions that seem to have a correlation to increased leads and sales.

Measure the Movement

We returned to our communication to influence model (look again at Figure 1.1). What can be measured *between* the steps? What actions would our target audience have to take to demonstrate that they now are *aware* of us, to indicate they now *understand* us, and to show they are *committed* to taking action?

For example, for staff and physicians, we measured:

- **Awareness:** email open rates, website visits, video views, and town hall attendance.
- **Understanding:** quantity and quality of questions, and tenor of comments online and in meetings.
- **Commitment:** managerial reports and feedback and measurable actions such as training session sign-ups.

The bottom line is that the Kaiser Permanente Colorado team judged our integrated communication program to be a success. The measures we took throughout the preparation and launch of the ACA exchanges showed ever-improving responses to our activities, ever-improving satisfaction with the organization, and ever-increasing sales.

Conclusion

More and more, corporate communication is integrating public relations, internal communication, advertising, and marketing. Not every organizational chart has the functions reporting to a single leader. But even when they don't, successful companies emphasize close coordination between the two functions by sharing goals and mapping out strategies together.

I personally have found it most effective to consolidate the disciplines into a single team. That makes it easier to allocate resources: when the functions are separate, it is unlikely that resources are shared, even if it makes strategic sense. I have led integrated teams at two universities and one healthcare organization, and in all three cases, my teams were able to continually improve their results even though budgets were stagnant.

I believe my experience in journalism, media relations, and on-the-job training in branding and marketing enabled me to be a leader who has a broad, knowledgeable view of the full spectrum of communication and marketing. But being a leader involves so much more than technical expertise.

Key to being a good leader is to be what's called a "systems thinker." I wish I had read Peter Senge's *The Fifth Discipline* early in my managing career. I became much more effective once I discovered that the problem in front of me today would continue to bedevil me unless I diagnosed the root causes. After I had diagnosed many systems issues, I began to recognize patterns and got better at untangling problems I'd never seen before.

I urge my students to be curious. Everything they learn in school today is subject to revision tomorrow. The only way you can keep up is to ask questions and follow the blog posts of people who are scouting the territory ahead of you. Don't be afraid to try new things. I have told my team members that failure is okay, as long as it was calculated and you learned from it.

I believe this is an opportune time for people to enter the corporate communication disciplines of PR, media relations, internal communication, advertising, and marketing. So much change is happening that there never will be a dull day for the foreseeable future.

What's more, it's easy to follow your passions. Just about every industry needs the special skills that we communicators bring. I have students who choose a PR career so they can work in the gaming industry, professional sports, music and entertainment, environmental activism, and social justice.

It's a great profession to do good by being good.

Steve Krizman
Associate Vice President of Marketing and Communications
Assistant Professor, public relations and journalism
Metropolitan State University of Denver
Denver, Colorado
skrizma1@msudenver.edu
@SteveKrizman

CONSUMER/LIFESTYLE PUBLIC RELATIONS

Erik Perez

Erik Perez is the principal public relations executive at Hello PR in Los Angeles, CA. With more than 15 years of experience in public relations, marketing, and branding, Erik founded Hello PR Group in 2014 to provide a unique and personal approach to public relations to help clients reach their goals.

Prior to launching Hello PR Group, Erik was managing director at HL Group (in both Los Angeles and New York), where he focused on home, design, and lifestyle clients. During his tenure at HL Group he was instrumental in the planning, development, and implementation of strategic communication, social media, and marketing initiatives for his clients, which included Crate and Barrel, Kelly Wearstler, Ligne Roset, Donghia, Bespoke Global, Cisco Home, Waterworks, and Caruso Affiliated.

Part I: Personal

After graduating from college in Mexico with an international business degree I had a wide range of odd jobs, from working for a customs broker in San Diego doing import/export to being a DJ on a Spanish radio station. The last of the odd jobs was working for a Mexican beef company in Los Angeles in their import/export department to Japan. It was there I realized that I was very far from what I wanted to do in life and began exploring possible career opportunities, ultimately discovering PR.

I began looking into possible ways to get my foot in the industry, but since I had no PR experience, and had been in the workforce for almost five years, my options were limited. The more I looked into it, the more I realized that I needed to go back to school. I decided to get a master's degree in communication from Boston University, with an emphasis in public relations.

After completing the program, one of my colleagues connected me with HL Group, a fashion, lifestyle, and consumer agency in New York. At the time, the agency was looking for freelancers for Fashion Week—an exciting experience as a first real PR position! After Fashion Week my freelance job ended and with no other job, and living in a tiny apartment, I just kept going to the HL Group office. During this time I tried to make myself useful by answering the phone, making calls, working on media lists, and arranging samples, and from here I was also able to tap into their resources. After a few weeks of showing up, one of the partners at the firm offered me a position as his assistant/coordinator for the firm's new home and design division (the "home team," as we called it). Since this was a new area for the firm it was just the two of us working with a few interior designers and home brands. Working at a large agency meant I was doing the work, while he guided. Thinking back, this was exciting and terrifying at the same time—and was really the best way to learn how to do things and what not to do. I learned several valuable lessons after a couple of lecturing email replies from editors, including one from the then editor in chief of *Elle Décor*, on how a new color way is not really "new."

As the HL Group grew, the home team also grew and we started working with more consumer brands with national recognition, including Crate and Barrel, CB2, Ligne Roset, J.C. Penny, Bed Bath and Beyond, and Kelly Wearstler, to name a few. This experience was wonderful and New York was exciting, but after a couple of years in the city, I had started thinking about a move back to the West Coast. While waiting for a client on a conference call, the firm's partner and I started talking about the possibility to move back to Los Angeles and help grow the home team in the LA office. A few months later, after two members of the LA team left, I moved to Los Angeles.

I was lucky enough to retain most of my clients, including Crate and Barrel and Ligne Roset, but I also started working on clients outside of the design category including many lifestyle brands and companies—which after years of being in my little design bubble and dealing mostly with shelter publications, was a wake-up call.

After almost five years in the Los Angeles office, and working on a variety of consumer, design, and lifestyle accounts, including a menswear fashion brand, a real estate development company, and a couple of civic and cultural institutions, HL Group was still interested in growing the design practice. In order to do this, we met with a number of great interior designers and up-and-coming brands, but when talking about the budget, I realized that design in Los Angeles was not at the same scale as in New York, particularly postrecession. Because of the demands on our office, we often referred the businesses to smaller PR agencies as we went after larger, more lucrative clients.

It was during one of these conversations that the light bulb came on: "Wait, why are we passing on this business? Why can't I be X, Y, or Z person that we are referring business to?" After a few weeks of thinking about it, I decided to leave HL Group after almost 10 years to start Hello PR Group.

I gave HL Group three months' notice—in part to end on good terms, since I was hoping they would send some business my way, but also to really think about what I was doing and how I was doing it. I realized there was more to consider and understand than just opening my computer and start sending emails. I started (and still am) learning and researching different business, legal, and financial matters that I never thought I would need. What is an LLC? What was an S-Corp? Do I need Quickbooks? It all became overwhelming at times, so I was glad I had the three-month buffer before I left HL Group.

The beginning was a bit scary, but luckily, just two days after I made the announcement public on social media, my first new business inquiry came through Facebook. The brand was a start-up in the home category looking for representation.

I've always known that PR was about relationships, but it really wasn't until I was on my own when I realized just how important they really are. It's not simply about knowing who the clients are, but really about developing close personal relationships. Even before I officially started Hello, I started telling my plans to a few of my contacts. They then shared my details with their contacts and in less than three months I had lined up five clients all in the design, consumer, and lifestyle areas, including a start-up company, BottleCloth; a Chicago interior designer, Julia Buckingham; and an Australian designer and author, Jason Grant.

Today, we are a team of five—four based in Los Angeles, and one team member in New York. We are all passionate about design and architecture, which makes what we do more enjoyable. We are currently working with nationally recognized home furnishing brands like Knoll and iconic California-based Heath Ceramics, as well as architects and interior designers, some of which have been included in prestigious lists such as the *Architectural Digest* AD100, the *Elle Décor's* A-List, and *LUXE Interior + Design Magazine's* Gold List.

Part II: Case Study in Consumer/Lifestyle PR

In 2015, Hello PR was engaged by a luxury consignment site for high-end home furnishings,[1] a new online marketplace for gently used home furnishings, to support the launch of its services to the West Coast (Los Angeles and San Francisco).

We began working with the company when it was going through its second fundraising campaign, which meant that the budget for the LA market expansion was minimal. The company was relatively new, and at that moment only serviced the New York tri-state area, so for the brand the goal was mainly to create awareness of its services in a new market, Los Angeles. Additionally, they were hoping to engage local interior designers to consign product on the site—ideally having five designers on board by the time of launch and at least three to five regional media placements by that time. To maximize resources, we developed a comprehensive six-month plan inclusive of intimate prelaunch dinners with select media and interior designers, one industry launch event, industry cultivation and introductions, speaking opportunities, and media outreach.

---

1. Due to privacy and acquisitions, the company name has been removed.

As a first step, we worked with the company to develop and refine their press materials to properly communicate the brand to the West Coast market. At the time, they were very New York–focused, and we needed to explain the benefits of selling and buying home furnishings through the company and highlight the difference between this company and similar online platforms, such as 1st Dibs, Craigslist, and Chairish.

Our first audience was the interior designer community. We wanted interior designers and architects to not only be aware of our services, but to learn how they could use it as a tool to either sell unused inventory or furniture, and as resource for last-minute client needs. To introduce the site to this audience, we developed a series of three intimate dinners with 12 to 15 attendees. These events were hosted by the brand's CEO and CMO, and intended to create a personal relationship, explain first-hand what the company is, and create excitement for the brand prior to the expansion. As a result, approximately 40 percent of the interior designers who attended these dinners became active users of the company by the time of the West Coast launch, either consigning product or purchasing items for their clients. The success of these small dinners was due to the relationships that were developed and the trust that was established between the brand and the users. Interior designers felt comfortable with buying and selling pieces on an online platform now that they had met the people and knew the process.

As part of the campaign, we were also able to connect the brand's CEO with the team at the Pacific Design Center in Los Angeles and secured her as a panelist during West Week. West Week is one of Los Angeles' leading trade events for interior designers, and there the CEO was able to speak about the intersection of design and technology, further positioning her as a leading voice in the industry and the company as a key resource for the industry.

Additionally, Hello PR supported the brand with its launch event in the summer of 2015. It was planned that the launch would happen the evening before Legends of La Cienega, a national industry event attended by interior designers from across the country and covered in national media. Hello PR worked with the company to organize all event logistics, planning, and on-site support and media outreach, securing *Traditional Home*, one of the country's leading home and design publications, as a media sponsor for the event. The event was covered by a number of national publication and blogs, which positioned it as the opening events to "Legends."

From a media standpoint, the West Coast expansion of the company was covered by a variety of regional outlets, including *C Magazine*, *Angeleno*, *Interiors California*, *Architectural Digest*, PureWow, Curbed, *LUXE Interiors + Design*, *InStyle*, and the *Los Angeles Business Journal*. As a result of our partnership, the company received more than 15 million impressions through media, resulting in an approximate media value of $140,000. The overall budget for this project was approximately $10,000, including the launch event and the three dinners.

Part III: Professional Advice

There are three things that I would like to leave you with. The first is about relationships. During graduate school I learned many things about PR on a general scale, but after graduating, I learned the importance of establishing relationships with editors. Having started at a small team within a large agency, I was lucky enough to have a hands-on learning experience and that allowed me to develop relationships with editors on a daily basis. The most important thing is to make sure that your relationships with editors are honest and genuine. As a first step, study the outlets you're reaching out to, learn what journalists and editors write about, who they write for, and how they write, and put yourself in their shoes: "Is this relevant for him/her?" If you do this, they will value your efforts and be more likely to respond to you. I can honestly say that one of the reasons why Hello PR is successful is because editors trust us. They know that when someone from our team reaches out on behalf of a client, it's because it's relevant to them and that we're not wasting their time and clogging their inbox with random pitches.

The second key thing I want you to know is about the value of PR. Not everyone will understand. After starting my own agency, I realized more and more that a big challenge Hello PR faces is having to educate clients on the value of PR. Many times they see the end result but don't understand the process, or they falsely believe that results happen overnight. In addition to wanting immediate results, a majority of clients have unrealistic expectations of what the results will be. And many times, they don't have a clear idea of what their goals are (or should be). These are the cases that are usually the most challenging. As part of the education, we practitioners need to always be transparent and guide our clients through the process—whether good or bad.

A final recommendation for any aspiring PR practitioner is to be resourceful and be aware of what's going on—not just in the industry that you're practicing in. You want to have a grasp on other industries and stay informed. Legislation, trends, and technologies are changing at a faster speed than ever, so the more we research and are aware of these changes, the easier it is to adapt. Even though our focus is consumer and lifestyle brands (let's be honest, we're not changing policy or saving lives), all these aspects affect the way we think about our daily work, how we approach business, and how we can better serve our clients.

Erik Perez
Principal/Founder
Hello PR Group
instagram @helloprgroup
twitter @helloerikperez | @helloprgroup
facebook.com/helloprgroup

3 INTERNAL COMMUNICATIONS IN PUBLIC RELATIONS

Jasmine Myers

Jasmine Myers is a first-generation college student, Boriquen, divorcee, single mother to two strong-willed girls; a Californian, a dreamer, people person, empath, coffee-lover, photographer; raw, transparent, Christian, a multitasker, sister, and friend. She is also account manager for Power PR, an agency support-ing B2B clients in a broad range of industries includ-ing security, retail, manufacturing, and industrial. Jasmine's career started as a graduate student at the University of Southern California, twisted through entry-level PR positions and a career in advertising, and finally ended in a place that suits both sides of her experience.

Part I: Personal

Born in the early 1980s in Carson, California, my family sought more affordable housing 80 miles inland to San Bernardino, California. My parents provided us with a stable, two-parent, lower-middle-class home that placed a great value on our education and time spent together. My father worked as a graphic designer in the aerospace industry and my mother was our primary caretaker.

My brother, sister, and I attended public schools in San Bernardino, but because we were Gifted and Talented Education (GATE)-identified, we enjoyed smaller class sizes and the commitment of some stellar, pas-sionate educators. As a young student, I was praised for my writing skills and competed frequently in oral poetry contests and creative thinking improvisations.

Ultimately, I graduated high school sixth in a class of 598, over-coming a lot of adversity on my path leading up to that point. Late nights in the public library tapping into the free Internet and not owning a home computer until grade 11 was not reason enough to prevent me from not exceling academically. I enrolled in every ad-vanced placement class offered by the school and took a couple of col-lege courses at the local community college during the summer of my junior year. I considered psychology or economics as college majors but didn't have much exposure to different career paths. I just hoped everything would make sense once I got to college.

Sociology: Valuable Preparation for a Career in Public Relations

I remember the day I received my letter of acceptance to Occidental College, one of nine colleges to which I applied. I was offered a Trustee Scholarship, along with several grants and local community scholarship awards, putting a college education within my reach.

I entered Occidental College as a first-generation college student with an undeclared major, declaring sociology during my second year. I was able to apply a substantial amount of credits toward my degree from a handful of community college classes, combined with credits earned from excellent scores on the advanced placement exams I had taken in high school as well. In May 2005, I graduated from Occidental College with a Bachelor of Arts in sociology, a year ahead of schedule at the age of twenty-one.

Looking back, my degree in sociology served as an excellent springboard for entering the world of business but didn't offer me the practical knowledge I needed to actually step into a position at an agency and do public relations. It was clear to me during my senior year of college that additional training or certification would be needed in order for me to work in public relations.

A journalism professor encouraged me to consider public relations after inviting me to shadow a couple professionals at the *Los Angeles Times*. Professor Sipchen took an interest in mentoring me as soon as we realized we had graduated from the same high school; a kinship had formed, as it wasn't often that I ever crossed passed with anyone from San Bernardino in my new circle at this prestigious liberal arts college. Professor Sipchen described public relations as "a perfect blend of a love for writing, with an interest in business," and after a day shadowing one of his PR colleagues at the newspaper, I too was convinced I would enjoy the field and I set off to pursue it.

All in all, the sociological perspective I gained during my undergraduate education proved to be valuable preparation for my career in public relations. Insights into social factors like race, gender, ethnicity, age, education, and social class have been crucial for working in today's multiethnic and multinational business environment. These insights have been helpful while crafting messaging tailored to resonate with certain niche audiences. Additionally, many of my sociology classes developed my ability to dissect and draw conclusions from large quantities of statistical data, a skill set that has been very helpful in my ability today to decipher the return on investment (ROI) of a campaign for a client. This mindset also helps when honing in on a particular group targeted in a campaign and better identifying the needs of different demographics, thus customizing my tactics to reach them with my message accordingly. Sociology has, in a sense, afforded me the background to practice smart, informed public relations that is sensitive to the varying needs of a diverse marketplace.

The Fast Track to PR: Grad School for the Working Professional

Immediately following commencement from Occidental College, I entered University of Southern California's Strategic Public Relations program as the youngest student in my cohort. Ranked #1 by *College Magazine* for the study of public relations, a degree in public relations from USC Annenberg is invaluable. Coupled with the value of the "Trojan network," my degree from USC translates to employers that I am a strategic thinker, a strong communicator, an accomplished writer, and a professional with high potential.

USC's graduate program in strategic public relations prepares graduates not only for rewarding jobs in a variety of industries, but empowers them with the leadership skills and adaptability to navigate a profession that is constantly changing. Upon graduation, USC PR students are hired for their ability to hit the ground running with expert writing, multimedia and digital production, social media, and strategic planning skills, and they are promoted quickly in their careers for their ability to analyze campaign outcomes, conduct original industry research, and use theory to inform future thinking. This was certainly true for me, and I credit much of my success in the fast-paced agency sector to the training I received as a graduate student at USC.

Designed to be completed in conjunction with full-time employment within the field of public relations, the program's training launched my career in PR. The school's network of alumni is almost as valuable as the curriculum itself, and before my first day of class, I had successfully landed a three-month internship at a reputable crisis communication agency. The agency was owned by a female PR practitioner, Agnes Huff, who had been in the business for over 25 years. Her clients were diverse, from nonprofit organizations to a multimillion-dollar manufacturer of toilet accessories. While interning for Agnes Huff, I learned the ins and outs of monitoring press coverage, proofreading press releases and media advisories, and how to support an agency's account team members with various administrative and research tasks.

Graduate classes were held in the evenings, and discussions were incredibly fruitful as my classmates were working professionals with varying levels of expertise in the field. I was a sponge, soaking up the knowledge served to me every day over the course of those two years. Each class was taught by a PR practitioner with real-world experience and skill sets. As the students, we were able to tackle case studies and problems in class, accelerating my learning over the course of the program's two-year curriculum. If I could go back to those times, I would have taken advantage of the program's international opportunity for students to work abroad for a semester in either South Africa, London, or Hong Kong. However, I chose to stay local that semester, to be near family and friends.

When my internship ended, I accepted a full-time position as an assistant account executive at Productivity Public Relations, a boutique public relations agency located in Hollywood that focused primarily on consumer product PR in the juvenile, toy, and novelty good products. Within six months, I was promoted to the account executive level. I managed the PR and media relations for approximately eight clients under the direction of the agency's vice president and current owner (who is currently one of my closest mentors), including Joovy Baby Products, Delta Children's Furniture, and the Preservino Wine Preservation System. It was in this intimate, boutique agency environment that I really learned how to craft the art of pitching and build a strong media list using Cision and manual Internet research. While email pitching was critical to communicating my clients' brand and products, following up with editors via phone was invaluable to my relationship building with editors and success in placing my clients in those publications.

I would encourage all new PR practitioners to not rely too heavily on email communication, and to personalize their pitches as much as possible, every single time. As a young practitioner, I kept a communications log noting personal details about top editors, so as to reference them before reaching out to them in order to hopefully land another media placement. Editors receive calls all morning long, so anything I could do to differentiate myself from the pack was a good thing. In retrospect, working in a small agency such as this one was really an amazing thing for my career, as I was able to hear more senior account team members on the phones pitching. I could indirectly shadow them day in and day out, accelerating my understanding of the art of pitching and media relations. I had to be really creative in my pitching strategies as my clients were mostly start-ups, with brand names that editors wouldn't recognize. Instead of riding on a large, well-known brand name, I had to communicate their relevance and newsworthiness to the editors with succinct, tactful communications skills and messaging.

My Accidental Stint in Advertising: A Time of Exponential Career Growth

Upon graduation from my program at USC, I applied to a position at a PR and advertising agency in Orange County called O'Leary and Partners. The agency's largest, most lucrative account was in the motorcycle/power sports arena. I was hired in as an account executive to work on the Kawasaki Motors account, along with a seasoned account supervisor and VP account director. As you would have it, just as soon as I accepted the position, the agency lost the PR focus of the account. The agency was then only responsible for the creative development of the account's national advertising initiatives—commercials, print ads, product photography, racing collateral, and retail point of purchase creative. I had absolutely no formal education or training pertaining to the world of advertising, but the agency was willing to put me on the fast track to learning the business.

I have to admit that I was in over my head that first month in my position, and rightly so. Not only was advertising entirely new to me, the agency was much larger than any I had worked in previously and I knew nothing about power sports and motorcycles.

They say that it is in times of challenges and discomfort that we learn the most, and that was certainly very true for me in this position. I rose to the challenge—I was a hungry graduate.

I was, as it turns out, quite the project manager, and my previous public relations pitching skills served me well as I presented creative concepts to the client and managed talent at events and photo shoots. I was often sought out by copywriters at the agency to proof their work, and even brought in to brainstorm messaging concepts with the copywriters once they realized I was a strong writer. Within six month's time, I had propelled myself forward into the senior account executive role and was traveling quite frequently with the client and head creative talent to industry events and shoots for large campaigns. I was forming relationships and learning so much, managing a project budget of over $2 million annually.

In this role, I learned the importance of becoming an expert in one's field and portraying a sincere interest in understanding a client's products and audiences. Many of those in the business rode motorcycles to work, rode dirt bikes on the weekends, and spent long weekends in the summer buzzing around large bodies of water on jet skis. They lived and breathed the products they were promoting.

In order to gain respect and a seat at the table in a predominantly male industry, I drew from my sociological background and did my best to understand this subculture by immersing myself in it as much as possible. I took a class to learn how to ride a motorcycle. I started attending bike rallies in my down time. I organized trips with coworkers at the agency to local dirt bike and jet ski destinations. I earned a lot of rapport from the client by doing this, and gained valuable insight into what messaging would resonate with them for my projects because I understood the audience so much better.

In PR, for me now as a more seasoned practitioner, this is still crucial for my success. We must know our clients and our products, and have a pulse on the latest things trending in our industry. In this power sport advertising position, my understanding of advertising agency lingo and formal training was less important than my knack for people and my ability to dive right in and submerse myself into the culture of my client's company. Don't just do your research online. Experience your client's business as much as possible, and it will translate into authentic messaging and broaden your ability to creatively approach their business challenges.

Going Internal: Leaving the Agency Sector for a Corporate Position

After a two-year stretch at the ad agency on the power sport account, I was exhausted. Sixty-hour workweeks had caught up to me, and I wanted a better work–life balance. I assumed a position at Toshiba America as a business-to-consumer (B2C) project manager on the creative services team within the marketing communications department. The creative services team served as an internal agency of sorts for the corporation, staffed with copywriters, designers, and project managers. I worked hand in hand with product managers and retail marketing managers to develop marketing collateral to support each of the company's quarterly product launches.

I reported directly to the VP of marketing communications in this position, who was also a graduate of the Annenberg School at USC. He trusted me with a $1.3 million budget and highly visible projects, and I credit a lot of that opportunity to the loyalties of the Trojan network.

In this project manager position, my main responsibility was drafting creative briefs for marketing collateral and messaging briefs for new products. I would collaborate with product managers and listen to the concerns of large retailers like Wal-Mart and Best Buy and decide how to tailor our sales messaging in creative marketing pieces to meet those needs. I helped develop product packaging for laptops, displays for retail end-caps in stores, event pamphlets, sell sheets—anything consumer-facing was managed by me.

Another large part of this position was managing not only internal creative team members, but also external venders and contractors. This is where many of my public relations skills came into play, as interpersonal communications were pivotal to my ability to relate to these vendors. I would give them direction on the projects they were spearheading, and also compared bids from various agencies to find efficiencies for the department. Maintaining consistency of our brand and messaging across all channels and vendors was also my responsibility in this position. It was a big job, with a lot of exposure—but it felt so slow-paced that I realized I was missing the hustle and bustle of agency life.

After four years at Toshiba America, I found out I was expecting my first daughter, Faith Avery. I opted to part ways with my corporate position and focus on my family. Every now and then I would take a freelance gig to keep my public relations skills and relationships current, but focused most of my energy on my then two daughters and trusted that I'd enter the workforce full time when they were both in school full time. My husband worked a demanding schedule, and I embraced my new role as a mother to two little girls, 20 months apart.

Back in the Agency Saddle: Industrial Public Relations at a Glance

Four years later, after the onset of a divorce, I made the decision to re-enter the workforce full time a little sooner than expected. I had hoped to stay home with my children until they reached kindergarten, but in such a fast-moving industry and in the wake of new life circumstances, I knew it was in our best interest for me to get back into the agency saddle, relocating my daughters and me to Los Angeles for more opportunity. I expanded my job search to include Los Angeles—one of the PR hubs of the country.

Shortly thereafter, I applied for and accepted an account manager position at a PR agency in the South Bay area of Los Angeles called Power PR. The agency aims to help companies with newsworthy products grow and expand by delivering the highest quality and largest volume of news articles and features stories about their product or service to generate leads and sales.

The agency's model utilizes news articles about a client's products and services to increase public awareness, name recognition, product visibility, and sales. Based upon a belief that the public relations industry is often not held accountable for concrete results, it is the only PR firm that I have ever encountered that guarantees its clients a minimum of three to five published articles per month—and delivers on that promise.

The agency team consists of two principals, a sibling duo, in addition to account managers, media relations specialists, and high-tech journalists and technical writers with backgrounds in such fields as computer technology, electronics, medicine, engineering, manufacturing, retail, and education. With over 30 employees dedicated to providing its clients with the best PR for their industry-specific needs, I joined the team as one of four account managers. While public relations is primarily dominated by women, this agency specializes in fields that are primarily male, which made for some interesting parallels between this position and the one I previously held on the power sport/motorcycle account years earlier.

As an account manager, I manage a roster of eight to 15 clients at any given time. As soon as the client signs the agency's contract, I become their main point of contact. Essentially, I work to further educate the client about our strategy, recommending a list of publications to which we should pitch our feature story. I work to coordinate all interviews for the story development, interacting with the client and their selected story participants, which are often customers.

Part II: Case Study in Internal Communication PR: SK Enterprises

An Overview

A recent report identified that United States retailers are losing $60 billion a year to inventory shrinkage. Choosing to defend against theft is a necessity for businesses looking to reduce significant losses due to theft and shoplifting.

For 52 years, my client (dubbed SK Enterprises for the purposes of this case study) has developed and manufactured innovative asset protection systems that maximize return on investment for its retail and industrial customers. SK Enterprises works with retailers to reduce shrinkage caused by shoplifting through an extensive catalog of security solutions and custom products. Additionally, SK Enterprises provides solutions for displaying merchandise and creating safer environments, all while not inhibiting customer interaction with products in-store.

From electronic alarm modules to sensors, CCTV domes, safety/security mirrors, and recoilers, SK Enterprises provides affordable solutions to its customers. It keeps costs down by controlling the manufacturing process from concept to completion within its three state-of-the-art manufacturing facilities located in Illinois, Indiana, and Michigan.

SK Enterprises offers a variety of products that allow for the display of merchandise while defending against theft. The primary categories are electronic alarms, mechanical security, and general security devices.

The Objective

SK Enterprises contracted the services of my PR agency to conduct a print marketing publicity program designed to generate high-quality published articles in appropriate publications in volume over time. The goal of the published articles was to increase brand awareness for SK Enterprises' products in North America, and to position our clients' products as a strong solution to a growing problem: retail shrinkage.

To do this, we worked tirelessly to publish a quantity of credible, third-party-supported articles over time in many trade publications in order to generate qualified leads that our client could turn into sales. These articles could also be reused once they were published to generate even more leads, to speed our client's sales process, to engage customers via social media channels, and to generate additional future business.

In addition to our article writing and placement program, we conducted a unique direct e-promo program for SK Enterprises. Combined with the ease of data distribution due to email, our email program involves a mass distribution of client materials (website, a turnkey feature article, actual published articles) directly to the client's prospect lists to get the promotion message directly and quickly into the hands of qualified prospects. We do this to generate a steady volume of leads.

How the E-Promo Works

We begin by creating a carefully worded email that does not seem like an ad or spam promotion and we send it out. This is a short email of three to five sentences designed to attract attention and encourage the prospect to reach back to us for the material we are teasing, such as a feature article we wrote, our client's website, a published article, a case study, tips sheet, or some other news. The most important part of this email is not so much the body content but the subject line, as most recipients decide whether to open and read an email based upon how well the subject line grabbed their attention. The subject line should speak to the recipients "point of pain" and in less than eight words, communicate how this point of pain may be addressed. For the case of SK Enterprises, the point of pain and the benefit of its products would be "reduce retail shrinkage with these loss prevention products and boost revenue."

When the prospect reaches back for this information, we deliver it. We then capture the prospect as a lead and immediately forward it to the client for sales follow-up.

It is critical that this piece not look promotional, in order to maintain third-party endorsement credibility. It's the same article that we are working to publish or have already published. In this way, we are not seen as directly or shamelessly plugging a product or service. Instead, we are simply inviting the prospect to read the article we have created (which in itself is designed to appear objective).

Some level of repetition best serves the e-promo program over time. For this reason, the sending of information is repeated until the item begins to pull a dwindling quantity of leads. Then, we create a new teaser email cover letter, swap out subject lines, and we continue our distributions. Although we change the teaser email, the actual deliverable (typically the article Power PR writes every three months) is the same each time. The e-promo is sent to the same main market categories and we will use industry codes (SIC codes) to reach this target via email. In the case of SK Enterprises, its main market segments are:

- retailers/merchandisers (all categories: department stores, electronics, hardware, clothing, accessory); and
- loss prevention professionals.

The Investment

The client was guaranteed three media placements per month, in addition to three monthly email sends, for a rate of $5,500 per month. Our agency is unique because it guarantees the client a certain number of media placements per month, or they receive a full refund. The contracts are month-to-month and no client is locked into a three-, six-, or 12-month retainer contract, which is common practice in public relations. It is almost unheard of for an agency to guarantee a certain number of media placements per month; however, my agency has done so for the last 25 years.

The Strategy for SK Enterprises: Month by Month

Month 1: Story Development and Becoming an Expert in Our Client's Industry

The first month's activity consists of research, setting up the feature article, selecting the publications to target for placement, and coordinating the collection of any necessary art, graphics, or photos needed to present the first story to editors. The process consists of the following steps:

- **Thoroughly research SK Enterprises market and competitors.**
  This is done to establish strengths and weaknesses, positioning, and to reveal market opportunities and threats. This action is ongoing, but up front it takes on a particular emphasis prior to any stories being written.
- **Initial selection of publications for the audiences we are targeting for the first story.** The list will be sent to the client to review. There is a detailed list profiling each publication including circulation, editorial content, and other pertinent data. Our media list for SK Enterprises is comprised of approximately 80 publications, all trade industry publications in loss prevention, retail merchandising, and retail operations.
- **The first story is assigned to a writer, who will conduct any additional research needed to complete the story.** This research includes, but is not limited to, calls to the client by me, as the account manager, for clarification on technical aspects of the product; quotes to be used for the story; additional resources within the company that might be appropriate to interview; and customers that are willing to be interviewed to obtain quotes. The writer, client, and myself work hand in hand to create a feature story that can be placed without much manipulation by the editor at any given media outlet. The idea of a completed feature article is unique to many other public relations agencies that typically pitch an idea for a story, rather than a completed one, or simply distribute a press release that is perceived as highly advertorial in nature. It is this provision of a complete feature story that I believe allows our agency to guarantee a set number of placements per month for its clients.
- **Work to secure art, graphics or photos that can be used for the first story.** A preference should be made to incorporate photos of the products in action, or in use in the field. Captions of no more than 30 words will accompany each photo and communicate to the reader the benefit of the products discussed in the feature article.

The story idea for SK Enterprises first feature article is "Loss Prevention Devices for High-End, Interactive Electronics." For retailers of high-end electronic items such as cell phones, pads and tablets, digital cameras, and drones, customers often want to interact with these items. They want to feel them, handle them, touch and manipulate them. However, as high-end items, retailers need to be able to allow this interaction without letting merchandise walk out the door due to shoplifting and even employee theft.

Electronic loss prevention devices are the ideal way to display this type of merchandise. The article will go into the component parts of the system and paint the picture of a variety of options available for different kinds of products. We quoted our client on the topic of loss prevention and types of products available, as well as quotes from two participants who utilize our clients' products in their retail for electronics.

Month 2: Pitching, Pitching, and More Pitching!

During the second month of service, emphasis is placed on devoting time and energy to contacting each editor on the publication list and convincing them to use the story in their publication. This is a rather intensive activity with dedicated communication between our media relations specialists, account manager, and editors.

Our specialty is contacting each editor personally. I craft carefully scripted oral pitches, which are used to determine if an editor is genuinely interested in carrying our piece. I do not send out unsolicited stories or press releases. I continue to personally follow up with each editor until I receive a verbal confirmation that a story or release will be used, which I then designate as a scheduled article, communicating that to the client accordingly. I continue to follow up with editors until the story appears in print.

During the second month of work for SK Enterprises, we opted to write a new version of the article: loss prevention of high-end clothing/accessories. This article paralleled the first feature article but introduced the issue of high-end clothing and accessories that clients want to try on. The elements of interactivity were different, and we focused on those differences. Our story also included two customer quotes from participants that could speak to loss prevention issues specific to clothing/accessories.

Month 3: Continued Media Follow-Up

In the third month, I continue to follow up and schedule articles for the first story. During this time, I continue to update my client on a regular basis and provide monthly reports regarding the overall status of the account by listing those publications that have scheduled or published our stories, along with their circulation numbers and a descriptive profile of the publication. Whenever possible, I provide the client with a clipping or an electronic PDF of the published story for their records and possible use in future marketing initiatives.

Gauging SK Enterprises Success

While only guaranteed three placements per month, Power PR placed SK Enterprises stories in a total of 48 publications in 12 month's time, with about 60 percent of the placements being in print publications rather than online editions. The client has seen a 13 percent increase in revenue in the first six months of partnership with us, doubling that success to an approximate 25 percent increase in revenue in the last year. Their website traffic has seen a significant increase in the last year and they've improved their search engine rankings significantly since partnering with our agency.

Our success was primarily in our editorial coverage for the client, but our email promotion efforts generated a total of 20 new leads for them—four of which translated to contracts with new customers.

Jasmine Myers
jasmine@jasminemyerspr.com
www.jasminemyerspr.com

4 HEALTH COMMUNICATION IN PUBLIC RELATIONS

Christina Trinchero

Christina Trinchero is currently the marketing communications director at Cooley Dickinson Health Care in Northampton, Massachusetts. In her nearly 20-year career at Cooley Dickinson, Christina has managed marketing, public relations, digital strategy, and strategic communications for Cooley Dickinson, a 140-bed nonprofit community hospital and its affiliated provider practices.

Part I: Personal

Who Am I?

I'm honored to be included in this collection of public relations case studies featuring PR practitioners. By the very nature of my work in PR, I talk more about others than I do about myself. But I recognize the importance of being able to respond effectively when confronted with the "Who are you, and what do you do?" question.

We live in a world where attention spans are shrinking and the constant buzz of our surroundings often signal distractions at every turn. Knowing your own story and being able to articulate it succinctly targeted to your audience—think personal elevator pitch—can set you apart. No matter where you are on your educational path, I encourage you to think through and be able to recite your story. Be proud of it. Refine as you go along. And enjoy the journey.

I earned a Bachelor of Arts degree in English/writing from the University of Massachusetts Dartmouth and a Master of Arts in communication from the University of Hartford. I'm currently pursuing accreditation in public relations through the Public Relations Society of America (PRSA).

So, You're an English Major

As an undergrad, I remember well-intentioned family members and friends asking which major I had chosen. The conversation often went something like this:

> THEM: So, what's your major?
> ME: English.
> THEM: Ah. You're going to teach, right?
> ME: No, I don't think so (while thinking, slightly panicked: *Am I supposed to?*).

Why did people automatically assume that majoring in English meant I would teach English? My father was a teacher, so maybe that was part of it. I admire teachers. I'm sure you can think of a standout teacher or coach who made an impact during your formative years. For me, teaching was always, and continues to be, a profession that interests me. But I wasn't immediately drawn to it as a twenty-something new grad.

In retrospect, those conversations unknowingly helped my career discovery process. Yet I soon learned that a degree doesn't define you. A degree in English— or any degree for that matter—opens doors to numerous opportunities. Author and professor of English Daniel R. Schwarz writes in his blog: "English majors choose a major that not only challenges them intellectually but gives them pleasure. They love to read and think that reading matters." Perhaps this resonates with you.

Schwarz offers an answer—justification perhaps—to a question I often grappled with as to why I chose English as a major: "What an English major brings to career possibilities is the ability to think critically, speak articulately, write lucidly and precisely, and to read powerfully, deftly, and with understanding of subtleties and nuances. They know how language works and have the written and oral skills to communicate effectively."

From Classrooms to Meeting Rooms

For new grads in the early 1990s, jobs were hard to come by. Waitressing and some freelance writing helped pay the bills while I searched for permanent work. Thanks to a friend of a friend, I landed an entry-level job at educational publisher Prentice Hall/Simon & Schuster. That job was the foundation for many important skills such as learning how to work as part of a team; understanding product deliverables and deadlines (vs. "flex lines"); increasing my emotional intelligence to enhance my interpersonal relationships with coworkers; navigating business travel and logistics; establishing credibility and trust; and developing my confidence in writing, speaking, and collaborating with others.

What's Familiar Again: My Current Job at Cooley Dickinson Hospital

I never thought that a volunteer position I held as a teenager would provide a sneak peek into a career many decades later. Realistically, it was the location of where I volunteered—as a junior volunteer in a hospital—that stuck with me. Later, the familiar feeling of that environment motivated me to apply for a position that I have held for more than 15 years.

Transcending decades, the experience of working in a hospital surrounded by talented people whose personal and professional mission is to take care of others now has meaning. I am one of those people taking care of others through my work as a marketing communications director.

It is a privilege to represent hundreds of doctors, nurses, housekeepers, lab techs, administrators, and other hospital workers through words, images, and stories. Broadly, I help the nonmedical community—patients, family members, donors, government officials—understand the importance of the well-educated, skilled, compassionate, and caring medical community at their local hospital. By the nature of my work, I also help influence how the media represents health and medicine, and continuously try to improve how my organization is designing effective health communications for the people we serve.

Challenges, Opportunities, Surprises

With any major challenge or change comes opportunity. That's how I viewed my switch from educational publishing to health communications. My biggest challenges boiled down to learning a new industry, adapting to a new work culture, and building relationships. That's not to say I didn't experience a learning curve, but knowing my audiences, communicating clearly, and having an open mind served me well during my many transitions.

I have always been motivated by deadlines, but working in PR I quickly learned that my to-do list could be upended suddenly to manage the unexpected. Glen M. Broom and Bey-Ling Sha write in *Cutlip & Center's Effective Public Relations* (11th ed.) that "writing planning scenarios is the art of anticipating and describing the range of possible future states. In fact, a common type of planning scenario involves anticipating the worst things that could possibly happen to an organization; this is crisis planning." Broom and Sha cite communication scholar Kathleen Fern-Banks, who summarized the need for planning: ". . . Successful crisis communication depends on crisis anticipation and thorough planning as well as open and honest policies with stakeholders and the news media." In healthcare, imagine the worst that can happen and it will likely will happen. If you're interested in crisis communications as part of public relations management, you'll find hundreds of case studies online and in chapter 9 of their book.

Looking Inward: Consider Your Internal Clients

My clients have always been internal to the organizations I've worked for. In fact, our marketing communications team is in essence an internal creative agency that supports a management team of nearly 100 people. These relationships require a customer-service approach to solving a variety of communications problems.

Here's a snapshot of three projects that have surfaced in the past few months:

- The infection prevention team requested a campaign to educate staff about the importance of frequent hand-washing.
- The cardiologists needed help planning their annual healthy heart lecture series.
- The childbirth center team earned an international designation called Baby-Friendly from Baby-Friendly USA, a program of the World Health Organization and the United Nations Children's Fund (UNICEF). The benefits of this award needed to be communicated to the community and the leadership of the hospital wanted to celebrate the employees' work in earning the global designation.

Each example above presents a unique communications partnership opportunity with a different client or team. The infection prevention team sought to raise awareness about the importance of hand-washing (clean hands save lives!). The cardiologists know that one tactic for acquiring new patients and fostering relationships with existing patients is to offer free lectures on timely topics such as heart disease in women and new blood pressure guidelines. The childbirth center staff were proud of the Baby-Friendly designation they had earned after years of policy changes and staff and patient education improvements. Publicizing this designation could help more women choose the center for their maternity care.

Part II: Professional: Two Health Communication Case Studies

Author's note: The first case study presented illustrates the four steps of public relations planning, known as RPIE, which involves:

1. Research/analysis of a situation;
2. Planning, goal/objective setting;
3. Implementation/execution/communication; and
4. Evaluation.

Case Study 1: A Campaign for Better Conversations About End-of-Life Care

You've likely heard the expression that nothing in life is certain except death and taxes. It's a statement usually attributed to Benjamin Franklin, one of the founding fathers of the United States, who wrote in a 1789 letter that "Our new Constitution is now established, and has an appearance that promises permanency; but in this world nothing can be said to be certain, except death and taxes."

Most of us don't think about death unless or until someone close to us dies. Death—and how each of us confronts it—is a uniquely personal experience that can be grounded in cultural and religious values. Yet studies suggest a commonality that connects us all is the fear of death and dying. As Earnest Becker writes in his book The Denial of Death, "The idea of death, the fear of it haunts the human animal like nothing else."

A woman from western Massachusetts understood this fear. During her life, Evelyn worked in the fields of publishing, library science, industrial psychology, and career counseling.[1] A positive impression of hospice during her mother's end-of-life experience led Evelyn to her last career as a certified bereavement counselor. Evelyn volunteered as part of Cooley Dickinson Health Care's Patient Family Advisory Council, a committee made up of patients and family members that work with the health care system on improving care and the care experience.

Evelyn's wish was to encourage others to proactively plan for the end of their lives. This planning would allow one's wishes to be known to their family and medical providers if the person was unable to speak for themselves at end of life.

Evelyn asked: How can healthy adults become more comfortable planning their end-of-life care? Her focus was to encourage conversations about end of life when people are healthy. These conversations, she suggested, could help people plan their death as if they would any major life event.

Evelyn died in 2015. She is memorialized in her obituary as an optimistic and joyful spirit, whose unending passion for life and her basic human kindness gave inspiration to her family, friends, and colleagues.

In her honor, friends and members of her local medical community organized a series of community-wide book readings and discussions based on the *New York Times* bestseller Being Mortal: Medicine and What Matters in the End by surgeon and *New Yorker* writer Dr. Atul Gawande. What a fitting tribute to Evelyn: reading the book and discussing its themes as a community could bring people together to start conversations about planning for end of life. (You can read a review of Dr. Gawande's book here: https://www.nytimes.com/2014/11/09/books/review/atul-gawande-being-mortal-review.html.)

---

1. Author's note: I use Evelyn's middle name in this case study because after multiple attempts I am unable to locate a relative to request permission to print her full name.

FIGURE 4.1 Book display for *Being Mortal*.

Problem Statement/Opportunity

Gawande's acclaimed bestseller *Being Mortal* has started a national conversation about the deep flaws in our society's current treatment of aging and dying people. Using his book as a springboard and drawing on the resources of Cooley Dickinson Health Care, we looked at our goals for end-of-life care and began to plan how to bring about better outcomes for ourselves and our loved ones.

Research: The Rationale for Planning for End of Life

Is there such a thing as a good death? An Internet search of the terms "aging" and "death" returns thousands of results ranging from scholarly articles to first-person narratives. Specifically, a public television documentary points fingers at the medical profession, noting that it is "often untrained, ill-suited, and uncomfortable talking about chronic illness and death with their patients."

Planning for the end of life is "increasingly viewed as a public health issue, given its potential to prevent unnecessary suffering and to support an individual's decisions and preferences related to the end of life," the Centers for Disease Control and Prevention recommends. The CDC explains:

> Just as promoting health and quality of life is a major public health focus, so too should be helping to ensure that the time leading to the end of life is in keeping with the individual's wishes and as pain-free as possible. A public health focus on death with dignity and with one's wishes honored is the logical extension of public health's efforts to promote well-lived, healthful lives. Advance care planning can help make that goal a reality.

A Campaign for Better Conversations About End-of-Life Care

After Evelyn's death, a committee of doctors, nurses, and administrators from Cooley Dickinson and librarians from 13 towns and cities in western Massachusetts began planning community-wide book readings and discussions.

The events were held in March and April of 2016. Libraries hosted the events and medical professionals facilitated the discussions. Publicity was targeted to library patrons and others seeking information about planning for end of life, hospice doctors and nurses, chaplains, people living with serious illness and their family members, hospital donors and philanthropists, and community opinion leaders. In late April 2016, Cooley Dickinson sponsored a culminating community lecture, which was the final event of the month-long series of community discussions. Two physicians discussed the needs of people living with serious illness and how to advocate for them. The lecture attracted adults of all ages and backgrounds.

Information about the campaign goals and objectives, the target audience, timeline, and more are presented here.[2]

CAMPAIGN GOALS

- Prepare community members for the later stages of life.
- Inspire discussions between community members and their medical providers.
- Familiarize people with local resources related to death and dying.

CAMPAIGN OBJECTIVES

- Help 100 participants better prepare for the later stages of life.
- Host or participate in at least four community events that facilitate discussions between community members, doctors, nurses, and other medical professionals by April 15, 2016.
- Create awareness of local resources related to advance care planning, including familiarizing at least 20 people with a healthcare proxy form by hosting an outreach event in Northampton, Massachusetts, by April 29, 2016.

TARGET AUDIENCES

- Library patrons and others seeking information about planning for end of life.
- Hospice doctors and nurses; chaplains.

---

2. A note about goals and objectives: the four-step process of PR planning or RPIE—research, planning, implementation, and evaluation—differentiates between goals and objectives. The PR plan I wrote for this project also differentiated between the two. According to the *APR Study Guide* 2017 (p. 23), goals are longer-term, broad, and future states of "being." Objectives focus on a shorter term than goals and define (1) what opinion, attitude, or behavior you want to achieve from specific publics; (2) specify how much change you want to achieve from each public; and (3) tell by when you want to achieve that change. Objectives should be SMART: Specific – both action to be taken and public involved; Measurable; Achievable; Realistic – or relevant or results (outcome) oriented; and Time-specific.

- People living with serious illness and their family members.
- Donors.
- Community opinion leaders.

TIMELINE/BUDGET/MEDIA OUTPUTS

- The planning committee met five times from December 2015 through May 2016.
- The community book reads were held in March and April 2016 with a culminating community lecture and outreach event in late April 2016.
- Budget: $5,800 covered the cost of advertising; an anonymous donor gave $3,000 to purchase copies of *Being Mortal* for area libraries.
- Media outputs: 436 people attended events; 30 people took healthcare proxy forms at outreach event; 3 newspaper articles written; 2 opinion articles written; 1 radio interview; 1 television interview.

EVALUATION

- Took attendance at community book readings.
- Distributed evaluation forms.
- Distributed healthcare proxy forms.
- Hosted debriefing event for event planners.

ATTENDEES' COMMENTS ON EVALUATION FORMS: WHAT DID YOU LIKE ABOUT THIS DISCUSSION?

- Hearing personal stories.
- Shows the importance of conversations before illness.
- Honesty and openness when talking about challenging and deeply personal issues.
- Sharing strategies for caring for loved ones.
- Small group discussions.
- Learning about options and resources for end-of-life care and planning; how to navigate through what can be a difficult time for a patient or family member.
- Opportunity to contribute: it meant a lot.
- Involvement of doctors and nurses.
- Multiple requests for more programs.

By encouraging adults to plan and begin to discuss about their end-of-life wishes with their healthcare providers, the Campaign for Better Conversations

Table 4.1 Measuring Program Effectiveness Against Objectives

Objectives	Measurement
Help 100 participants better prepare for the later stages of life	• 13 libraries in 13 communities hosted book readings. • ~100 people attended 10 book readings • 140 people attended the culminating community lecture. • Attendees were primarily baby boomers, people born between 1946 and 1964 who were providing care to their aging parents while also beginning to think about their own mortality. There were also some students who attended and people in their 80s.
Host a minimum of 4 events	• Doctors and nurses moderated 10 book readings/discussions. • 140 people attended the culminating community event.
Host outreach event in Northampton	• Nurses distributed 30 healthcare proxy forms and spoke with interested community members at outreach event held in recognition of National Health Care Decisions Day.

*According to the Massachusetts Medical Society, a healthcare proxy form is a simple legal document that allows you to name someone you know or trust to make healthcare decisions for you, if for any reason and at any time you become unable to make or communicate those decisions.

provided a valuable service to the community. As part of the evaluation of the campaign, we noted evidence of continued awareness and sustained interest. According to Cooley Dickinson's chaplain and other leaders in the faith community, there was no evidence in specific changes in end-of-life wishes. From a community relations perspective, the campaign strengthened partnerships between local health providers and libraries and improved name recognition for Cooley Dickinson and its medical staff members who presented at the community events.

Writing in *Cutlip & Center's Effective Public Relations*, authors Broom and Sha state that "the strategic management process involves four steps: research; planning and programming; implementation (of actions and communications), and evaluation. By conducting research and analysis as the first step, strategic management represents the open systems approach to public relations, whereby the organization takes stock of its environment. Contrast this to the closed systems, reactive approach, whereby the organization simply implements actions and communications without research, planning or evaluating."

As a PR practitioner, you may be involved in developing a communications plan as illustrated in the previous case study. You could be driving the process or comprise part of a team that is leading the communications charge. You could be asked to focus on just one aspect of that plan, for example. In this case, you are working in a complementary capacity, as an integral piece of a larger whole. Regardless of your contribution, it is important to think strategically. Consider using the RPIE process to guide your approach to any communications opportunity.

The next case study exemplifies working as part of a larger initiative. It demonstrates the need for practitioners to be flexible yet strategic in the skills they lend to a communications opportunity. I was brought into a project that had been ongoing for more than a year when I was asked to edit an opinion editorial (an op ed) and submit the editorial to a local newspaper.

Case Study 2: From the Frontlines of Care: Cooley Dickinson Addresses the Opioid Crisis

In western Massachusetts, deadly and near-fatal encounters with heroin, oxycontin, fentanyl, and other opioids are alarmingly familiar to EMS first responders and Cooley Dickinson Hospital Emergency Department personnel.

Like many communities across Massachusetts, Hampshire County's cities and towns are not immune to the opioid epidemic. There is national consensus that the overprescribing of pain medication fueled the current opioid crisis. Overprescribing began in the 1990s, when concerns about under treatment of pain became prominent. Many people who are addicted to heroin once used prescription opioids to manage pain. Today they are struggling with addiction.

From January 1 through September 30, 2016, 25 people died of heroin overdoses in Hampshire County, up from 17 deaths in 2015. The number of heroin overdoses in the city of Northampton, where Cooley Dickinson Hospital is located, has nearly tripled in the last year, according to data released in January by the Northampton Police Department. The *Daily Hampshire Gazette* reported that the police department responded to 51 overdose calls, 41 of which involved heroin overdoses. Some people were revived thanks to drugs like the FDA-approved naloxone, which reverses overdoses, saves lives, and offers second chances for some.

Opportunity

In 2014, clinicians from Cooley Dickinson started thinking about their role in facilitating second chances. They created an internal committee, the Cooley Dickinson Opioid Task Force, and joined with local law enforcement, local public health specialists, community clinicians, and first responders to form Hampshire HOPE (Heroin/Opioid Prevention and Education), a multisector coalition addressing the rise in prescription opioid misuse, heroin use, addiction, and overdose deaths in Hampshire County through policy, practice, and system change.

In addition, data compiled from Cooley Dickinson's community health needs assessment report reinforced that substance use is a problem in the region served by Cooley Dickinson and that there is community support to address the issue. This community support was also identified as a priority in Cooley Dickinson's strategic planning process.

To create awareness of the coalition's work, representatives from member agencies were invited to submit an op ed article to the *Daily Hampshire Gazette/* Gazettenet.com, the local newspaper and online news source for area residents. The November 2016 article "From the Frontlines of Care: Cooley Dickinson Addresses the Opioid Crisis" was written by Jeff Harness, MPH, director of community health, and Peter Halperin, MD, director of integrated behavioral health from Cooley Dickinson. Harness and Halperin are also cochairs of the Cooley Dickinson Opioid Task Force.

Objectives

- Inform the public and increase community members' knowledge that Cooley Dickinson is working on the opioid use problem.
- Set expectations that area residents who use Cooley Dickinson Health Care can expect to see changes over time in how care is provided and outline those changes that will be forthcoming. For example, in the future patients who come to Cooley Dickinson's Emergency Department will be asked screening questions related to substance use. Currently, Massachusetts law mandates specific steps for diagnosis and screening of patients who are suspected of opioid overdose. Another change will require that opioid prescribers educate patients on how to safely and securely store and dispose of unused medications.
- Demonstrate to the wider community that the collaborating agencies are taking the issue seriously and are motivated to make meaningful changes within the community to help prevent overdoses and deaths.
- Communicate in a positive way that helps to reduce stigma against people living with substance use disorders.

Program Planning and Strategy

Coauthor Harness described the process of writing the op ed as a collaborative one, and took the lead by writing the first draft of the piece. While familiar with the opioid epidemic and the impact the crisis was having on the community, Harness interviewed Dr. Khama Ennis, an emergency department physician and medical director of the Cooley Dickinson Emergency Department, to better understand the frontline realities of the problem.

"While the data tells the story of how we as a community are being impacted by opioid overdoses, Khama's first-hand accounts of patients she has treated humanizes the issue and explain the seriousness of what we are dealing with," recalled Harness.

Coauthor Halperin, a psychiatrist with Cooley Dickinson Medical Group, an affiliated physician practice, provided a historical and evolutionary view of the epidemic and addressed the stigma that is typically associated with substance use. It was important to let our community know that we didn't wake up one day and have a spontaneous crisis on our hands. The epidemic is a result of systemic, unintentional failures built on each other over time. Halperin notes in the op ed: "As physicians, we were taught that the risk of addiction to prescription opioids had been exaggerated."

Aligning the efforts of the HOPE coalition and Cooley Dickinson's opioid task force, Halperin and Harness used the op ed to pose the question, "What can you, our community, expect from Cooley Dickinson?" This, in effect, got our campaign rolling. The article deliberately answered that question with a series of steps that the community could expect from Cooley Dickinson and the community-wide HOPE partnership. It encouraged area residents to join local agencies in fighting stigma, educating themselves and their loved ones about the dangerous path to addiction, supporting people in recovery, and never giving up hope.

Evaluation

Program evaluation included testimonials from community members and a summary of online metrics. Testimonials are a form of qualitative research, which provide an in-depth understanding of an issue looking at the how and why of an approach; qualitative research is not measurable, and can be subjective.

In an email, Melinda Calianos, director of the Tobacco Free Partnerships in Northampton, wrote:

> I had to write to let you know how much I enjoyed reading your article in the *Gazette* today. I've been an avid and loyal reader of the *Gazette* for many years, and I don't recall reading such a well written piece, perhaps ever. Thanks for sharing the information in such a readable, interesting, and clear way.

Of the opinion article, Northwestern District Attorney David E. Sullivan, cochair of the Hampshire HOPE opioid coalition, said: "Everyone who commented to me [about the article] was pleased Cooley Dickinson Hospital was actively engaged in helping stem the tide of overdoses and addiction." He also noted:

> Knowing our community hospital is taking so many positive steps in addressing the opioid epidemic let me know that our community is working on life-saving solutions.... The newspaper column about Cooley Dickinson Hospital's

efforts in addressing the opioid crisis gave me hope we can help people caught in the grip of their heroin addiction.... It takes a community-wide effort to tear down the barriers to treatment for people addicted to opioids. Knowing our local hospital was helping people meant a great deal to me.

As a stand-alone tactic, the op ed case study was difficult to evaluate. Yet we received anecdotal feedback from several community opinion leaders, one of whom is part of Hampshire HOPE.

Additional measurement data includes the following:

- *From the Frontlines of Care* was published in print and online on November 29, 2016. The print circulation of the *Daily Hampshire Gazette* is 13,500. According to the *Gazette,* on Nov. 29 there were 6,756-page views of gazettenet.com.
- The article was also posted on Cooley Dickinson's website, where there were 37 unique page views. Cooley Dickinson's LinkedIn page included 916 impressions, 15 clicks, and 8 interactions with an engagement of 2.51 percent. As this is the first time Cooley Dickinson has authored an op ed article as part of the HOPE coalition for the *Gazette,* this data serves as a baseline and can be compared to future published articles.

Connecting back to our initial objectives, these results demonstrated that Cooley Dickinson was informing the public and increasing community members' knowledge that the organization's doctors, administrators, and public health professionals are addressing the opiod addiction problem locally.

Both testimonials align with the authors' objectives to share information about how Cooley Dickinson is working on the issue of opioid use dependence. Respondents acknowledge the efforts taking place among the collaborating agencies. Both individuals react with compassion, thus addressing the goal of reducing the stigma often associated with substance use. If you consider that the strategic planning process in public relations involves four steps—research, planning and programming, implementation, and evaluation—feedback in the form of testimonials, in the instance of this case study, could be factored into future programmatic planning. Sound public relations planning doesn't cease after one advances through those four steps; it is a cycle of evaluation and continued improvements built upon refined goals and objectives that question how efforts will impact the public relations process and ultimately, how behavior is impacted and changed. *From the Frontlines of Care* met the objective of communicating information to increase knowledge, awareness, and understanding.

It is a long-term goal of both the HOPE coalition and the Cooley Dickinson Opioid Task Force to set expectations for how care is delivered for people dealing with substance use challenges, and to educate area residents in an informative, sensitive, and appropriate way. An op ed as one tactic of a larger communications initiative is part of a continued effort to increase awareness and understanding.

Op Ed Earns a Gold Lamplighter

The evaluation phase of any public relations program measures effectiveness of the program against objectives, among other assessments. For the op ed, evaluation came in the form of judging by fellow health communications experts. In 2017, *From the Frontlines of Care* earned an excellence in writing Gold Lamplighter Award at the New England Society for Healthcare Communications 26th annual Lamplighter Awards ceremony. According to the society, the Lamplighter Awards recognize outstanding marketing and public relations efforts. The category Excellence in Writing is defined as an original piece written or commissioned for a healthcare publication, professional journal, magazine, or newspaper. Note: the op ed was submitted as a singular tactic and not part of the Hampshire HOPE's larger communications plan.

Working Collaboratively

Cooley Dickinson is one of more than 25 participating agencies in Hampshire HOPE, a community effort made up of many organizations such as treatment centers, schools, the Northwestern District Attorney's Office, first responders, and local health departments.

While this op ed represented one part of the coalition's larger mission to help people and families struggling with opioids in Hampshire County of western Massachusetts, the tactic needed to align with other aspects of the initiative. The case study exemplifies a part of a larger initiative and how agencies can successfully collaborate. (You can learn more about Hampshire HOPE, its initiatives, tips for helping a loved one, and more at http://www.hampshirehope.org.)

Part III: Professional Advice

What Would You Change in Your Career If You Had the Chance?

For starters, had I the chance and the forethought, I would have taken a year or more off between graduating from college and joining the work force. Instead, upon graduation I immediately searched for that all-important first job. In retrospect, taking advantage of a gap year or pursuing a sabbatical would have exposed me to new challenges and new experiences and might have set me on a different path.

What Do You Wish You Had Known When You Were Just Starting Out?

I wish I better understood the power of networking. I passed up several opportunities to connect with seasoned ad agency executives and tenured PR pros. Through friends, these people were willing to help with an "in" at their companies, but I was shy and unsure of myself. In an age when professional connections are a common metric tracked by LinkedIn and other networking sites, it's okay to reach out to someone to make a career connection. Be authentic. State your objectives clearly. And if someone ignores your request, keep at it or move on to someone else.

What Advice Do You Have for Student Readers?

Here are my notes on diversifying skills in order to go into a career in PR.

Inventory Your PR Skills

If you are considering a career in PR, take stock of the key skills and abilities that are considered core competencies in the field. Writing in thebalance.com, a website for personal finance and career information, author Alison Doyle suggests that the traditional skills of writing and media relations "will never fade in today's fractured media market." But additional expertise in creating content for social media, research, analytics, search engine optimization (SEO), and time management, among others, are also essential tools in an aspiring practitioner's toolbox. As you assess the attributes you can bring to a new job or internship opportunity, be sure to inventory your strengths and note areas where you think you could improve.

Internships Are No Longer Optional

There is no time like the present to research internship opportunities. Internships provide hands-on work experience and opportunities for students to build professional connections. According to monster.com, employers "overwhelmingly point to an internship experience as the most important factor they consider in hiring new college grads for full-time positions." Check with your career center or speak with an advisor or coach to learn more about internship opportunities in your area.

Connect With a Mentor

The Public Relations Society of America, www.prsa.org, offers a mentoring program where you can partner with an experienced PR pro. For more information about mentoring opportunities, check out PRSA's professional interest sections that focus on issues, trends, and research in specific practice areas. (For more on the PRSA, also see p. 128.)

Develop Your EQ

Emotional intelligence (EQ or EI) is the ability to understand and manage yours and other's emotions. The *Harvard Business Review* article "How to Boost Your (and Others') Emotional Intelligence," written by Tomas Chamorro-Premuzic and Michael Sanger, offers tips for developing your emotional intelligence including how to turn self-deception into self-awareness, how to turn self-focus into other-focus, how to be more rewarding to deal with, and how to control your temper tantrums. (Read the full article at https://hbr.org/2017/01/how-to-boost-your-and-others-emotional-intelligence.)

Volunteer to Explore What Interests You

If you didn't take advantage of an internship in college, it's not too late. As a student or a mid-career professional, you can use volunteering as a springboard to PR. By donating your time, you learn the inner workings of an organization while offering your knowledge to a lean communications department, for example. Use this opportunity to explore career and personal interests, uncover hidden talents, build contacts, and make friends. You will feel good knowing you are helping others while gaining personal direction and clarity.

Career Success Awaits You

While writing this chapter and reflecting on the case studies I've presented here, you may notice that I refer occasionally to *Cutlip & Center's Effective Public Relations*. This text is listed on the Universal Accreditation Board's "Short Bookshelf of Recommended Texts" and is considered one of the go-to resources in the field of public relations. In chapter 2 of that volume, pp. 41–42, the late public relations executive and professor Richard Long lists "five qualities of those on the career 'fast track'" that provide an inspiring send-off here:

1. **Results.** The single most important key to success is a reputation for getting results, being goal-oriented.
2. **Conceptualizing.** Those on the fast track have an ability to focus on the employer's or client's needs.
3. **Human Relations.** Persons on the fast track are team players who balance personal goals with those of an organization.
4. **Style.** The most important style-related trait is a can-do attitude. Another is constructive competitiveness.
5. **Intangibles.** This quality almost defies description, but charisma, presence, and moxie affect the way other managers evaluate people in public relations.

So who are you and what do you do? Have you crafted your own story or is it still a work in progress? Regardless of where you are in your studies or in your career, I hope the case studies presented in this chapter – as well as the personal narratives and reflections interwoven throughout this book – offer both mental fodder and personal motivation to help you begin exploring your place in the PR profession. Best wishes in your studies and in building meaningful and effective relationships throughout your career.

Christina Trinchero
Marketing Communications Director
Cooley Dickinson Heath Care
Cooleydickinson.org
Tina21820@gmail.com

NONPROFIT PUBLIC RELATIONS

Jillian Kanter

 Jillian Kanter is currently the communications co-ordinator at Verrill Dana LLP, a full-service law firm with offices across the Northeast and clients around the globe. In that role, Jillian supports both internal and external communications for the firm's more than 130 attorneys in approximately 35 practice areas and industry groups. Taking both a reactive and proactive approach to public relations initiatives, she works to promote their practice based on recent trends, cases, or other pertinent information for current and prospective clients.

In addition to working for Verrill Dana LLP, Jillian recently graduated with her MBA from the University of Southern Maine and volunteers on development & marketing committee of the Ronald McDonald House Chari-ties of Maine and on the marketing committee for PROPEL Portland, which services young professionals in the greater Portland, Maine area.

Part I: Personal

So how did I get to where I am today? I have always loved working in teams, helping others, challenging myself intellectually, and—ask anyone who knows me personally—I love to communicate. I'm always talking, typing, texting, or writing. It is only natural that I became a communications coordinator. However, if you asked me 10 years ago where I would be today the answer would be a bit more complicated. When I was younger I had aspirations of becoming a chef, a teacher, or a writer. If you had asked me if I could see myself in PR, I would have replied with "in what?" It was not until my first internship after my sophomore year of college at the University of Connecticut that I really got a good grasp on what public relations was. While the industry has come a long way in terms of visibility over the last decade, the definition is evolving and that very sense of the unexpected is one of the many rea-sons why I love what I do. I did begin college with a major in marketing, but at the time, I was not really sure what that degree would result in. I had thrown around the idea of sales as I had watched my father over the years in his successful sales career, but other than that, I did not have a good picture of what would come after graduation.

My first internship was a far cry from the legal industry where I am today. I found out about the opportunity through a friend of my older sister's who had worked at the agency for a few years. After talking to her a bit about what public relations entailed, I decided to take a risk and apply. The PR firm was located in downtown Boston, Massachusetts, only a couple of streets away from well-known Newbury Street. I took the train in to town (three different ones each way) to experience PR—unpaid—for the summer. To many that might sound like a miserable way to spend a summer vacation at the age of 19, but I had a blast! I worked eagerly alongside my first set of PR mentors on projects that truly ran the gamut. One day I could be rushing across the city last-minute to collect design files from a community center client. The next day I could be assisting with media check-in and press coordination for a celebrity-filled golf tournament benefitting a cancer foundation founded by a former New England Patriots player. Some assignments were more exciting than others, but they all forced me out of my comfort zone.

While I did learn to draft media advisories and press releases, many of my early internship days were spent researching media outlets and contacts, and clipping media highlights for clients. At the time, I dreaded the hundreds of calls I would have to make to confirm contact information for our media lists. Despite my love of talking I hated making phone calls, even more so in front of a group of coworkers. All of the interns were seated at a large table in the center of the room, with more experienced PR professionals' cubicles circled around us. I would make phone call after phone call, and the process became a little easier each day. It took me a few years, though, before I realized that this dreaded but simple task was in fact an important step to the media calls and story pitches that would come to consume much of my time in my first few postgraduate positions.

Heading back to college with my newfound passion for public relations, I had a whole new outlook on my education and what I wanted to do following graduation. While it was too late to switch my major to PR, I declared a minor in communication studies and enrolled in as many relevant classes as I could over the next two years. Learning everything from consumer behavior to advertising strategies, I looked at each new subject differently and applied everything to my new dream job. The next summer, I decided to explore a new internship opportunity at a smaller PR agency just down the road from my home on the north shore of Massachusetts. Working with a smaller team, I was able to participate in even more aspects of PR for nationally recognized outdoor retail brands. I created and edited press materials, monitored media coverage daily, and learned how to compile monthly clip reports and e-newsletters distributed to clients. I also helped to plan and prepare various events, including new product launches, industry parties, trade shows, media dinners, and tours. I returned to intern again that winter and one last time temporarily after graduating from college to help train the newest set of interns, assist in business development research, and to continue with many of the responsibilities I had the summer prior.

When applying for my first full-time position, I could not help but remember what one of my first PR mentors had said to me about working with clients in an industry that fits the lifestyle you want in the future. While the first PR agency I had interned at had an impressive client list, it included many restaurants, nightclubs, and charity tournaments—all of which required night and weekend commitments in addition to the daily workload. As having a work–life balance is important to me, I kept this in mind when looking for opportunities both in the Boston area and in Maine. Although I did look for job listings online, the position I ended up accepting as an executive assistant at Broadreach Public Relations was unlisted. A small public relations agency located in downtown Portland, Maine, Broadreach's client list consisted mostly of financial institutions and professional service businesses, but also included some nonprofit organizations, healthcare companies, consumer brands and events.

From the start of the job-hunting process, I took the time to research each agency and company I applied to, the types of clients they had, and what I could glean of the company culture. I chose to work at a smaller firm because I valued the added experience I could get with my hands in a little bit of everything they did. One thing that helped me stand out from other applicants while on the job market was the print and digital portfolios I created to showcase my work, as well as the experiences I shared from my internships. While "executive assistant" was not my dream job title, I knew I wanted to work at the agency and could see the growth opportunities that existed there. Starting out as an executive assistant, I was able to work alongside Broadreach's president and founder, learning not only how she served clients from onboarding to reporting results, but also how she ran the small business. Despite the title, I was able to do quite a bit of public relations work for high-profile business clients throughout New England, and even led a website and social media development project for a nonprofit geared toward fraud prevention awareness. Finally, I was also afforded the ability to learn client operations, creating detailed hours reports and clip report packages, the later of which I continue to do.

It was only eight months later that I accepted the new title of PR assistant for Broadreach. In this role, I was able to start constructing full communication plans for client events, workshops, and sponsorships, as well as continue to pitch and place articles. It was at this time that I started to develop a good base of experience in corporate communications and public relations, working with a law firm similar to the one I work at today. As PR assistant I was also able to draft and place public service announcements as an additional tool for promoting nonprofit fundraisers and other initiatives.

In less than six months from my promotion to PR assistant, I received my second promotion to assistant account executive. In this new role, I began to take on even more responsibility in developing and executing targeted media strategies and expert visibility plans to help raise the profile of our clients in various industries locally, regionally, and nationally. I had switched to a more strategic role and began to take the lead on some of my own accounts. This brought me to my final role at Broadreach, account executive and client operations coordinator. In this role I not only took on more accounts, but from a client operations perspective, I also ensured all client needs were being met with the highest level of service and efficiency throughout the client lifecycle. During my nearly three years at Broadreach, I was able to help make a great deal of difference for our clients. It is hard to explain the excitement you get from a client when they see their company featured in a national newspaper, when they call to tell you that everyone has read their new article, or when they get to say their event is officially sold out. Those moments make all of the long hours and hard work you put in worth it.

At Verrill Dana LLP

From Broadreach, I continued on to Verrill Dana, LLP as their communications coordinator. At Verrill Dana I am responsible for both internal and external communications for the firm's more than 130 attorneys in approximately 35 practice areas and industry groups. Using a targeted approach, I engage a variety of channels and tools to reach different audiences with specifically tailored messages. For example, say a new wage and hour law has been announced that employers need to be aware of. I would work with the relevant labor and employment attorneys to identify which industry sectors might be most effected and create tailored content for media and association outreach, email marketing, social media, blog posts, podcasts, and speaking engagements within each industry. There is a lot involved in each project, and more often than not there is a short window of opportunity to get ahead. Like that of any PR role, the position requires you to master multitasking and big-picture thinking.

In addition to my role at Verrill Dana, I volunteer on the development & marketing committee of the Ronald McDonald House Charities of Maine, assisting with the planning and promotion of its annual gala, and as a board member of the nonprofit organization PROPEL Portland on its marketing committee. As Maine has the oldest population in the country, PROPEL Portland has an important mission to attract, retain, educate, and connect young professionals in the greater Portland area. The organization works closely with the Portland Regional Chamber of Commerce and a number of local businesses to host events and offer resources, such as the recently launched web application that pairs up young Portland professionals with peers looking to move to the state. My particular role on the board involves media outreach, event promotion, and other marketing support as needed.

I also served as the communications chair of the Maine Public Relations Council (MPRC) for three years. Another nonprofit organization, MPRC aims to promote the public relations profession in Maine and to support PR professionals on their journey to becoming an APR (accreditation in public relations). MPRC is one of only nine organizations in the United States that is part of the Universal

Accreditation Board (UAB), which oversees this important designation. As communications chair, I helped to promote the different initiatives and events that took place, such as a new membership drive, scholarship announcements, professional development events, and the annual conference. More specifically, this involved reaching out to other local organizations and media, calendaring events, and posting on MPRC's different social media channels.

Prior to joining its board, I was an active member of MPRC, assisting the annual conference and professional development committees in coordinating and promoting regular events that aligned with the knowledge, skills, and abilities tested through the APR exam. While it is recommended that you have five years of public relations experience before you begin the APR process, college seniors and recent graduates can now take advantage of the new Certificate in Principles of Public Relations, also offered by the UAB. More than 20 colleges and universities currently have programs for interested students. Taking the extra step to earn your certification early on can help you stand out from your peers when applying for your first job in PR. Whether or not you choose to apply for a certification or accreditation, I highly suggest becoming involved with a local chapter of the Public Relations Society of America or another PR group in your area. These organizations offer invaluable resources for professional development and networking throughout your career.

While not at Verrill Dana LLP or volunteering, I attended classes at the University of Southern Maine, and recently graduated with my MBA. Taking courses in everything from leadership to finance and accounting to marketing management, I found the program to be an invaluable experience. While it is crucial to learn and build expertise in the marketing and communication field, some overlook the importance of also understanding end business objectives and subject matter of the organization you are working with. These MBA classes have allowed me to build a deeper knowledge of how to define what business success is and how to measure it. They have also helped me to develop more confidence and leadership skills.

I am truly humbled by the opportunities I have been given working with such great clients and team members, as well as the success I have been able to achieve throughout my career so far. In 2015, I was honored to receive the Rising Star Award by the Maine Public Relations Council. Given once each year, this award recognizes a young public relations professional who has exhibited extraordinary achievement and outstanding work in the public relations profession. A year after that, I received the President's Award from the former Maine Public Relations Council president, who has been a tremendous guide and mentor to me throughout my PR journey in Maine.

While working at a PR agency can provide you with a well-rounded experience that you would not necessarily receive when working directly for a business or organization, there are some challenges. At an agency you are assigned multiple clients to service at a time, which can result in an overwhelming workload and pull you in many different directions at once. As is standard with most agencies, you would be expected to keep track of the hours, and sometimes minutes, spent on each activity to ensure you have not dedicated more time to the client than defined within the contract. There are also more barriers to go through in terms of setting up interviews, getting information from experts, and in just getting the approvals needed to move forward on a project. And, by nature, you do not have the intimate knowledge of the company or organization that you would as a direct employee. Recognizing the limitations that working in any agency can bring, I decided it was time to make the leap to corporate communications, which brings me full circle to my role today as the communications coordinator at Verrill Dana.

Part II: Case Study in Nonprofit PR: The Cromwell Center

Public relations strategies are crucial for nonprofit organizations to gain visibility and raise the funds they need to be successful in their missions. Furthermore, they understandably often lack the budget that their for-profit counterparts have, making it more difficult to execute their plans.

A nonprofit organization exists for every cause, illness, and religion you can think of. In addition, you have some universities, chambers, and professional organizations that fall into this sector. According to the National Center for Charitable Statistics, there are more than 1.5 million nonprofit organizations in the United States. When you take the country's population of more than 320 million, you have a nonprofit organization for every group of about 213 people. Each organization must break through the noise to reach their audience and further their cause or mission. With all that said, a well-thought-out PR plan can go a long way toward driving success and telling the organization's story.

While the definition of public relations in general can differ, in my opinion, the best way to describe nonprofit public relations is as fostering and growing the relationship between a nonprofit and the public, and more specifically with its donors and volunteers. Each nonprofit has a different mission, but most share two common goals: they want to raise funds and visibility for their cause or mission.

For nonprofits, public relations campaigns can be effective alternatives for achieving these goals, as opposed to more traditional marketing and advertising campaigns. This is in part due to the little to no hard costs associated with most PR strategies. These strategies also lend well to showcasing the nonprofit as genuine and trustworthy.

For example, say there is a local nonprofit geared toward childrens cancer research named Lucy's Corner. Their public relations campaign might involve three main strategies—media relations, social media marketing, and content marketing. All would focus on one main theme—telling and showing the story of Lucy, a child who overcame cancer and wanted to give back to the community, and other local children suffering from the same illness. Across strategies, Lucy's story and that of her peers would be shared using different tools and channels—articles, blog posts, media interviews, and social media videos. Each would contain an action that a viewer, reader, or listener could take to participate in the mission. These strategies all connect the audience in a seemingly personal way to those who would benefit the most from anyone who supports the organization. They also specifically state how one can get involved—an important piece to successful nonprofit PR.

In 2015, while working at Broadreach Public Relations, I had the pleasure of working with The Cromwell Center for Disabilities Awareness (The Cromwell Center) to promote its 10th annual dinner and auction. The mission of The Cromwell Center is to promote safe, respectful, and inclusive schools and communities. The Cromwell Center was named in honor of Jeremiah Cromwell, a resident of the Maine School for the Feeble Minded, who died in 1928 at the age of 14 and was buried in a nearly unmarked grave for almost half a century. The Center's goal today is to ensure that "no person with any kind of disability will ever again experience the profound isolation in life and anonymity at death of Jeremiah Cromwell." More information on the Cromwell Center for Disabilities Awareness can be found online at www.cromwellcenter.org.

Prior to sitting down with the organization's executive director for our kickoff meeting, I did my research. What had they done in the past in terms of PR for the event? Had there been any previous media coverage? What could I learn about the organization that would help me to understand its objectives? It is important to note that while you should conduct thorough research before the initial meeting, the messaging and PR plan should not be formulated until after you have met with the client. You should always be sure to ask benchmarking questions and learn more about what success looks like for them. This will allow you to develop a well-crafted plan and to measure your success in a meaningful way.

In 2015, the same year as the event, Broadreach Public Relations received a Gold Award for our public relations efforts surrounding The Cromwell Center's 10th annual dinner and auction at the Annual MPRC Golden Arrow Awards Ceremony. This case study highlights the success of the project and expands upon information included in Broadreach Public Relation's award-winning submission.

Background

For some more background, the annual event serves to not only help the organization promote its overall mission, but also to raise money for its free disabilities awareness and sensitivity programs offered to elementary school students throughout southern and central Maine, as well as the resources it creates for families and teachers. In addition, the 2015 event honored Maine native Travis Roy, who was presented with The Cromwell Center's Mission Award. Now a well-known advocate for disabilities awareness through his foundation, Travis is a former ice hockey player who experienced a tragic accident just 11 seconds into his first college hockey game, leaving him a quadriplegic. The event also recognized UNUM, an insurance and employee benefits company, for its longtime support with The Cromwell Center's Community Partner Award.

As a public relations firm, our goals for the project first and foremost were to increase awareness for the event and the organization as a whole. More specifically, our key objectives were to increase attendance; aid in the securing of 50 sponsors, including five new ones; increase both Twitter followers and Facebook likes by 50 percent; secure at least five pre-event stories; and lastly, to attract at least two media outlets to attend and cover the event. We also needed to accomplish all of this with a budget of only $5,000.

The main public relations strategies used for the project included a combination of targeted media relations and social media marketing. Given the existing reputation of Travis Roy in Maine and Massachusetts, we were able to pitch interviews with the honoree prior to and at the event in combination with marketing The Cromwell Center's story. Targeted pitches were made to journalists who had either written about The Cromwell Center or Travis Roy in the past, in addition to sports, education, and health reporters; local print and broadcast media; and Roy's alumni publications. Given that the event was hosted by and benefited a nonprofit, we were able to draft and secure the placement of a public service announcement on local television and radio stations to further promote the event. We also posted the event to online community calendars and asked local print media to share the event information in their listings. Lastly, from a media relations perspective, we invited society page journalists from both Portland and Boston, including the *Portland Press Herald*'s "Scene & Heard" page.

From a social media standpoint, we first searched relevant hashtags and social media influencers. Next, we developed a comprehensive posting plan, which outlined when and to which channels we would post to, in addition to what content each post would include. For example, the plan may have included a post to Twitter three weeks prior to the event date with a link to purchase tickets. Another post for Facebook that same week may have highlighted the honorees with a link to learn more about the event. Other posts linked to press coverage for the event and alternative ways to support the organization and its disabilies awareness and sensitivity programs. Posts would also include the relevant hashtags, with some posts tagging influencers in an attempt to expand the reach of our message. Lastly, we created a custom hashtag, #ChangeAttitudes2015, which was used on The Cromwell Center's social media pages leading up to the event and displayed on each table at the event to encourage more conversation. During the event, each attendee was also asked to visit the The Cromwell Center's Facebook page to take an online pledge against bullying by liking, commenting, or sharing the post that was pinned to the top of the page (see Figure 5.1).

We are dedicated to the purpose that no person with any kind of disability will never again experience the profound isolation in life and anonymity at death of Jeremiah Cromwell. Our mission is to change attitudes and build understanding so that people with disabilities can enjoy the same respect, support, and opportunity that we all deserve.

Pledge to Be Aware

I pledge to...
- Embrace the abilities of others.
- Act as a role model for generations to come.
- Stay positive and judgment-free.

FIGURE 5.1 The Cromwell Center Pledge.

In the end, more than 41 unique media placements were earned, including 25 stories that ran prior to the event held on June 7, 2015. All clips were positive and included our key messages. In addition, the local ABC (WMTW-TV) and CBS (WGME-TV) affiliates attended the event, resulting in coverage about the organization and an interview with Travis about his inspirational story. Other key placements included interviews in radio, blog, and print media. In looking at the total ad value equivalency of the earned media, we were able to determine a return on investment for the client of 853 percent.

Although we excelled in terms of media coverage, a few areas fell short. The event took place with just 48 sponsors, not the 50 proposed; however, we did meet the goal of securing five new ones.

With a goal of increasing The Cromwell Center's social media following by 50 percent, we had our work cut out for us. In the end, we increased the number of Twitter followers by nearly 14 percent and Facebook likes by just over 31 percent in a short period. While we did not achieve the full goal, we were able to see a spike in engagement. In particular, the online pledge reached approximately 1,900 people, with 33 likes and 31 shares.

While we did not meet all of our objectives in their entirety, we were able to help pull off a successful, award-winning event, reaching a record number of attendees and increasing the overall community's awareness of the organization.

There were some lessons to be learned from the project, as well, especially in terms of social media. The targeted increase in followers of 50 percent for each Twitter and Facebook was in the end unachievable in such a short time frame. Also, as a team, we took a creative risk in implementing the live online pledge. What we did not expect was perhaps a less social media savvy audience. Many of the pledges were posted following the event, instead of from attendees during the event. Reflecting on the project now, it may have been helpful to create a detailed profile of our target persona and their preferences. While we did increase awareness for the organization, by pinpointing who the ideal donor was more specifically, we may have diverted more of our efforts from social media to alternative channels, whether it be capturing pledges by hand or video taping them at the event for use in traditional advertising campaigns, on the website, and at future events.

To this day, this special event sticks out in my mind not only due to the successful public relations campaign executed by myself and the rest of the Broadreach Public Relations team, but also because we were truly able to help this organization to fund and bring awareness to such an important mission.

Part III: Professional Advice

One of my mentors told me a long time ago that it takes a special person to be in PR. Not everyone is cut out for it. Public relations is a field that continues to grow in popularity, yet is still not well understood. Many think that a career in PR is synonymous with attending fun parties and spending hours on social media. While events and social media can be important tools in a public relations strategy, the industry is so much more than that. PR can be both fun and rewarding, but you have to go into it with an open mind. Public relations is all about elevating another person, brand, business, or organization, and as a professional in this field, you tend to be behind the scenes. This behind-the-scenes work may come in the form of ghostwriting an article or crafting a quote for a press release, and is vital to the success of the campaign, but doesn't come with front-stage accolades. While everyone may not know that you were the actual author, the true gratitude comes from the success you are able to achieve for others, something especially gratifying in nonprofit PR. It is important to identify your objectives ahead of time so that you can truly showcase and prove that your hard work has made a difference.

As we are often behind the scenes, many people ignore or do not fully understand the important role that public relations has in shaping what the public sees and experiences. Take for example crisis communications. Building a positive reputation prior to a crisis can make or break the organization and how the community reacts to an often tragic situation. In addition, the course of action when responding to the crisis is more often than not led by a public relations team or professional. While PR professionals work closely with the leadership at a business or nonprofit, we are often the ones shaping the voice of the business or organization. This is why it is crucial for those in PR to advocate for a seat at the table. Without this internal trust, success will be harder to achieve.

In a similar vein, trust with your consumers and target audience is increasingly important to build. People are now taking the extra step to block out commercial messages and the voices of advertisers. They're flocking to new medium and paying for services that come free of advertisements. Reaching your target audience has gotten a whole lot harder, which brings both challenges and opportunities for PR professionals to showcase their skills and really raise the profile of the brands that they work with. As PR practitioners, our value comes from thinking outside the box to come up with innovative solutions to help our clients or companies achieve their objectives—whether they are to increase sales for a business or attract a record number of volunteers for a nonprofit. I cannot stress how important it is for someone in PR to keep up on trends in the industry, as well as what is happening in the world. Personally, I do this through a number of subscriptions to news and public relations email blasts, and by attending industry and local events. Many of my proactive ideas are inspired by something that I have read or seen, whether it is a new law that was enacted or a new challenge identified by someone in our target industry. Staying attuned each day is crucial, as the windows of opportunity may come and go quickly.

This brings me to my next recommendation: know and understand your audience. I cannot tell you how many times a client or prospect has told me they would like to be in the *Wall Street Journal* or on the *Today Show* or some other national mainstream outlet. Your role as a PR professional is to determine not only if this is actually achievable, but also whether or not it makes sense given the particular objectives and target audience. While a large number of readers or viewers is great, you might be able to achieve greater success through a more targeted medium, such as a trade journal or professional association. Do not stop at one outlet or one channel, however; *always* repurpose your content and pitch it and post it as many places that are relevant as possible. This is especially important for nonprofits, where repurposing can cut down on the time and cost that it takes to create entirely new content.

My final piece of advice is to stick with it. As an entry-level PR professional you will more than likely be required to do a lot of the grunt work and not play a large role in the overall strategies. These early experiences may be trying, but they are important as you work your way up the chain, gaining more strategic responsibility. Your days of completing small tasks will help when you take the lead on a new project and need to view it from more of a big-picture perspective.

In closing, I owe the success that I have been able to achieve so early on in my career to the diverse experiences I have had to date, the wonderful mentors I have met, and the true passion I have for what I do. My education, my internships, and postgraduate PR agency experiences have been invaluable in building the expertise that I need today and has helped me to secure my dream career path in public relations.

Jillian Kanter
Communications Coordinator, Verrill Dana LLP
Twitter.com/JillKanter
Linkedin.com/in/jilliankanter

6 COMMUNITY RELATIONS AND PUBLIC RELATIONS

Jack Pflanz

 Jack Pflanz is a communication and public relations professional specializing in MTH (making things happen). He is an award-winning publicist with experience in local, regional, national, corporate, nonprofit, government, technology, lifestyle, and culinary enterprises. He excels at strategizing, implementing, managing and coordinating, public relations, fundraising, and marketing campaigns and events. He has extensive experience with writing, pitching, and placing news stories with print, broadcast, and web-based news media outlets. Jack also has a unique stor. He follows the wisdom of the past, with his eye on the next generation. Jack pursues his passions and uses his PR experience to get him there.

Part I: Personal

My father used to say, "If you want to make God laugh, just tell him your plans." Well in my case, it was very true. I grew up the youngest of four siblings. Our father was an auto mechanic, tow truck driver, and gas pump attendant who worked long hours and never made more than ten thousand dollars a year in his life. He was functionally illiterate and never completed the eighth grade. At times, he was one of the wisest people I had ever known. We grew up in poverty, in housing projects, and in the poor part of a little town in Upstate New York called Utica. Food was a precious commodity. Many nights I went to bed hungry. This would be a big influence on my happiness, success, and relationship with my own daughter in the years to come.

Dad was a master problem-solver, it is probably why he was such a good mechanic. He loved puzzles. He had this knack for seeing the big picture. He was a firm believer in education. He pushed us all to work toward a better future. He used to say, "From the neck down you are worth minimum wage, from the neck up you are worth anything you want." My siblings and I have more degrees than a thermometer. I remember hearing him say "Everything happens for a reason, even if we never understand it." My mother passed away when I was fifteen;

I could not understand it, but years later I would. Without her income we struggled. At fifteen years old I went to work on the weekends in a large Italian restaurant. I worked thirty-plus hours in three days scrubbing greasy pots and pans, while going to high school, working on the school newspaper, and running on the school cross-country and track teams. I made $3.35 per hour, which usually came out to about $100 per week. I gave my father $75 for rent, food, and bills, and kept $25. This would be the basis for my life-long work ethic and for my desire to work in the culinary industry thirty years later. I figured out very quickly that my father was right. I was making minimum wage and the best way to make sure I had a better future was to start thinking and working from the neck up. The first step would be to get into and pay for college. The biggest challenge to that objective would be money.

The four of us siblings all put ourselves through college. We have a total of twelve degrees between us, including two masters degrees. While working up to three part-time jobs at once, I earned an AAS degree in media, marketing, and management from a community college. After taking a year off to work, I secured a full-time job as a student loan collections representative and attended a New York State University (SUNY) full time and received a BA in business and public management with a minor in marketing and communications.

The next challenge would be competition in the job market. In my junior year of college, I realized I was going to have the same degree as thousands of other people who were applying for the same jobs. I knew that I needed to somehow

FIGURE 6.1 Dad and me, Mohawk Valley
Community College graduation, 1989.

differentiate myself. While working full time and attending classes full time, I started my own advertising agency. I called it Solutions Marketing. I called on businesses that catered to college students. I arranged for them to advertise on college radio, college TV, and in college newspapers. I charged 15 percent commission on whatever the business spent with the school. It provided enough money to pay for books, and something unique to put on a resume.

After graduation, I moved about an hour east to Albany, and worked dead-end jobs for a couple of years until I moved back home to take care of my ailing father. It would not be until five years after college, in 1998, that I discovered the field I would work in for the next 20 years. Dad also used to say, "Do what you love for a living and you will never work a day in your life." He was right: I have had a passion for PR work ever since. I was working in insurance and volunteering as a public relations committee person for my local running club when I was asked to promote a local fundraiser. As a result of my volunteer efforts, I received my first job offer to work in PR.

My first job in public relations was in county government. I worked as publicist and speech writer for the Oneida County Executive. Public service was a great way to learn about demands, challenges, and rewards of working in communication. This experience in county government served as the basis for my relationship with local media contacts. I learned quickly that controversy sells newspapers, and to be very careful of what you say to the press and how it can be perceived. I also learned something that has served me well over the last two decades: relationships are key! I have spent years building mutually beneficial relationships with local, regional, and national news media contacts and influencers.

After government work, I went into the nonprofit field. I learned that nonprofit not only described the industry, but also the salary. I did not make much money, but I learned an awful lot about compassion, empathy, and relationship-building. I worked with the American Diabetes Association for four years, and it was the most fulfilling job I have ever had. I created and implemented a program where I recruited walkers and runners to complete 26.2-mile marathons and 13.1-mile half marathons in locations around the world in exchange for fundraising. This was perfect for me as I had been a runner for more than 15 years, I had quality relationships in the local running community, and knew the local media well. Also, I had completed two full marathons and two half marathons, so I had walked the walk and could talk the talk. As a part of this job I had the distinct pleasure of taking teams of people to marathons in Maui, Hawaii and Dublin, Ireland. You cannot not imagine what a thrill this was for a poor kid from the projects of a small town in Upstate New York.

I sent press releases and scheduled interviews with local TV and radio every time I held recruitment meetings, finalized a team to train to travel to a location, or when one of my participants had an emotional story about participating in honor of a friend or family member who suffered from diabetes. Media relations was my bread and butter as it pertained to runner and walker recruitment. In fact, one of my participants was a local TV news anchor who had just started running.

She signed up to run her first marathon after just having completed her first 15k race. She was determined to run the Walt Disney Marathon in honor of her father, who had passed away from complications due to diabetes. She used her platform as a local news personality to complete her fundraising goal of $3,000. She also convinced the station to run free public service announcements featuring her TEAM Disney teammates to help recruit for future races.

Prior to leaving for Florida, she informed me that she was bringing a camera man with her to take footage and combining it with footage she shot at training runs, meetings, and events, and the station would air a half-hour special about the program and the effects, symptoms, and signs of diabetes the night before her team ran the race. In the next few years I would use this segment as a recruitment video to build credibility with future participants. As I said earlier, it is all about relationships. I also used local media to promote local and regional ADA fundraising events as well as education, awareness, and advocacy programs.

This was the position where I learned about the news value of the nonprofit story, the art of the pitch, crisis management, fundraising tactics, and how to frame a story. Over four years we recruited approximately 150 participants and raised over $300,000. Aside from the New York City market, we were one of the most successful areas in the country. During my time as a fundraiser with the American Diabetes Association, the insulin pump was introduced to the mass market. Later, several of my walkers and runners would train with the pump. This device was made possible as a result of all of the fundraising done on behalf of the ADA. This is when I felt the program was a success.

As life progressed, it was necessary to move on to a better paying position. This was difficult, as I justified working so many hours for such little pay because I was helping people who lived with a disease. Now in an effort to help support a family (including a new wife and baby) and pay a mortgage on a house that was entirely too big for us, I was going to promote cell phones. I started out in the wireless technology industry in 2003 as a public relations specialist for a subsidiary of Nextel Communications, known as Nextel Partners. It was not long before I felt better about turning to the dark side (private enterprise). I was confident in my ability to build relationships with local reporters, write effective press releases, and highlight my new client (the office general manager) with local media. The bonus was that I was given a budget of about $100,000 for the year. I could use it to work with local social service and nonprofit agencies to build and maintain the community reputation of the company. I was also given the directive to come up with community and volunteer events, prizes for employees, and activities for the office staff to participate in, and then of course publicize our involvement.

There is a big difference between a for-profit PR budget and a nonprofit budget. With Nextel, I estimated an amount of money to spend annually based on market size, local office sales goals, and the number of strategic opportunities available in the market that would have the potential of a return on investment (ROI) for the company. In nonprofit you first estimate the gross amount you feel you will raise with events and fundraisers, calculate net income after expenses, and then backtrack to try to bring expenses to 10 to 20 percent of the net total. So, you might need to add more events or find ways to increase event revenue or decrease expenses to get to the desired percentage of expenses. Basically, your spending budget has a direct correlation to your fundraising and expense budgeting abilities. What it comes down to in nonprofit work is that every penny counts, so you operate on a frayed shoestring budget.

My position with Nextel broadened my experience beyond just local and regional news media. Another gem of wisdom from Dad came to mind. He would say, "Always try to be an asset and never a liability." It was here that I started to position myself as an information resource for reporters on a regular basis. I adopted the policy of checking in with my reporters and asking them if they were working on anything I could assist with, instead of only contacting them when I had a story to pitch or needed a favor. Before long, they were calling me (instead of my competitors) and asking for information, statements, products for reviews, and executive interviews. This practice led to mutually beneficial relationships with reporters in large metropolitan media outlets and many repeat stories. Soon, I became responsible for news media relations in several other states throughout the Northeastern United States.

At this point I was very happy professionally. I had a good job, a nice office, and good people to work with. The hours and days flew by. This was where I remembered what Dad said about not working a day in your life if you did what you loved. It was also at this time when what he said about God and my plans resurfaced. After working with Nextel Partners for four years, they were purchased by Sprint and became Sprint Nextel in 2007. As part of the merger, only one communications manager on the Nextel team would join the new company. Fortunately, I was the one who received the offer. So now in a blink of an eye I was working in the corporate communications department for a multibillion-dollar, international wireless communications conglomerate. This was a long way from the housing projects on the south side of town.

Throughout my next seven years I worked with journalists from news outlets such as the *Wall Street Journal*, the *New York Times*, *Business Week*, NPR, American Urban Radio Network, ESPN, CNN, ABC, CBS, and NBC national *Nightly News*, to name a few. I would also come to work with several celebrities, authors, and some of the most successful public relations firms in the country. I was not just pumping out press release after press release, I was planning and launching campaigns about communications programs in 42 states, arranging media tours around the country for professional athletes, setting up satellite media tours for award-winning authors, and winning my own national awards for my work. The lesson from this position was that the more work you can do on a story for a reporter, the better chance you had of not only securing one story but future stories as well. From 2009 until 2014 I had been laid off three times. Two of those times I was able to work my way back into the company through other divisions. In 2014 Sprint went through a massive work force reduction and I was out of work again.

Work–Life Balance

This is where things get interesting. In 2005, while enjoying my professional life, my personal life took a turn. I was going through a separation and divorce. I was going to be a single, divorced, working parent. I worked with my attorney over the course of two years and several thousands of dollars to ensure I would not be just another every other weekend parent. I was determined to have time during the week with my child and be a part of the everyday parenting process. I wanted to be a part of making dinners, helping with homework, assigning bed times, making breakfasts and school lunches, shopping for clothes together, going to the hair salon, going to doctor's appointments, going to recitals and school plays, and taking care of my child when they were sick or sad. My goal is, and was, to set a standard for how Morgan was to be treated by others in life. Ironically, it would be the divorce that would serve as the catalyst for the wonderful relationship we enjoy today and for the business we would start together.

While going through the divorce, I realized I was going to have to learn to cook. You see, I had this kid who was going to want to eat three meals per day for the next fifteen years. Kids can be so demanding that way! I started devouring everything I could find about cooking. I started watching the *Rachel Ray Show*, subscribing to her magazine, visiting her website, looking up recipes, and buying cookbooks. After a while, I fell in love with the culinary arts. I absolutely loved to cook and bake. I even wrote an email to Rachel Ray thanking her for all of the wonderful resources she offered and for basically teaching me to cook. As Morgan got a little older, we started cooking together. We would post pictures of our meals on social media, and as a result we would be inundated with recipe requests. One day Mo came home from school and told me that friends were not eating the way we were. They were going through the drive-thru every night of the week, after soccer or football or dance or baseball or basketball.

Wanting to spread our passion and way of culinary life, we came up with the idea of creating our own cooking show on YouTube. Thus, the Jack and Mo Cooking Show was born. We created and posted home videos of ourselves making fast, easy, healthy, inexpensive meals that families could make together. It soon became our mission to help families learn to cook together, eat together more, and communicate around the kitchen table as generations before us did. We came to love cooking together, formed a wonderful father–child bond, and learned a lot about food and healthier eating. It also served as a way for us to communicate together about everything happening in our lives.[1]

After making videos and cooking together for two years, we received a call from the *Rachel Ray Show*. They had seen our YouTube channel and had the email I had

---

1. You can enjoy our videos from our YouTube channel or our website www.JackandMoCooking Show.com. To view our appearance on the Rachel Ray Show visit https://www.youtube.com/watch?v=hxYrkm1clNU

sent them four years earlier. They invited us to be guests on the 1,500th episode. They asked us to make two videos. One was a video of us cooking one of Rachel's recipes (we chose to make dark chocolate bacon pancakes). The other video was a stand-up of us telling Rachel our story and thanking her for her help. It was at this point on national television that Mo thanked Rachel for teaching me to cook, since before that I could not boil water.

A week or so after getting the call from a producer we were on our way to New York City to appear on national television. It was quite an experience and certainly helped our credibility. Rachel and her staff were extremely gracious. Two weeks later I would be laid off from my position with Sprint for the last time. But what was going to come next was going to be exciting. With eight months of severance pay coming to me, I was sitting at my computer working on my resume when I started to get hungry. I went to the stove and started cooking one of our more popular YouTube recipes when it hit me like a brick of butter.

I thought there must be a way to monetize our love for cooking, help local families, create a business, and build the bond between Mo and I even stronger. So, after giving it some thought, I made an appointment with a local small business institute and began to brainstorm. I struggled with the type of food business I would start. Would it be a cafe, or maybe a catering service? I stared to hear my Dad's voice again and it reminded me of yet another saying he repeated over the years. He would say, "Give a person a fish and he eats today but if you teach a person to fish he eats tomorrow." With that, I would spend the next year looking for a new full-time job and working on a business plan for a family-oriented culinary education service (a fancy name for cooking school), to help families come together over learning to cook fast, easy, healthy, inexpensive dishes while communicating and enjoying meals together.

After being laid off from Sprint in November of 2014 for the third time and after conducting an exhaustive job search for almost a year, I decided to take matters into my own hands and do what I do best. Instead of only reacting to postings

FIGURE 6.2 Our logo, designed by Mo.

about open positions, I needed to be proactive. In October of 2015 I worked with a print shop and had a double-sided sandwich board sign made that announced I was available for hire. I rented the marquee of the local arts theater and displayed a similar message. I walked up and down the main business street for four hours while wearing my best suit and the sign with resumes in hand. One week prior I had issued a media advisory to local news outlets. The day of and in the days leading up to my march I conducted an interview media tour of the local morning radio talk shows. While I marched, I was interviewed by the local daily newspaper, the local AM news radio station, and a local TV news reporter. As I walked from the theater to the New York State Office Building and back, I used my cell phone to conduct a social media campaign and created hash tag #HireJack. My crazy stunt resulted in exactly one job offer to sell used cars, but more importantly, it gave me something local, unique, and relevant to showcase my skills during job interviews.

While job hunting, I still had my eyes on the prize of starting my own business. On February 16, 2016, we officially launched "The Jack and Mo Cooking Show." We began offering group and individual cooking classes, birthday party classes, live

FIGURE 6.3 Operation #HIREJACK.

demonstrations, and our own local meal prep delivery kit service. At the launch, I issued a press release to local media announcing our mission to help local families. As a result, our local newspaper assigned the story to a reporter and sent a photographer for a photo shoot. A few days later we were pleasantly surprised with a feature article about the two of us and our new business. As we started to schedule regular classes, we were invited to be interviewed by our local radio and TV stations.

In November of 2016 we were hired to conduct a seven-hour cooking demonstration during the grand opening of a regional department store chain. After that I started approaching department stores, and I was able to book us a job doing a three-hour demonstration with our local JC Penney. Word started to spread and we started getting requests from not only local business establishments but also from nonprofit agencies. Over Christmas we were asked to demonstrate a recipe at a holiday party at our local children's museum.

Word starting getting around in the community, and during the summer of 2017, we had the good fortune of being asked to offer classes at our local community college.

Part II: Case Study: Community Public Relations–World Hunger Day and Hunger Action Month

According to a report published by the New York State Community Action Association in February 2017, 43.5 percent of families with female head of households with children present are currently living in poverty in Oneida County.

The Problem

St. Margaret's Food Pantry is a mission of Grace Church. The ministry is a resource for people in the downtown geographical area who are in need of food supplies. The Food Pantry is a partner agency with the Food Bank of Central New York and is obligated to provide a minimum of three days of food each month to individuals who seek services. In the last few years, the pantry has provided more than 25,000 meals and served more than 2,500 individuals. State and federal cutbacks have made it difficult to continuously have enough food to help those in need. Food supplies constantly run low and assistance with replenishment to meet obligations is often needed.

Objective: World Hunger Day

Use the Jack and Mo Cooking show brand to help St. Margaret's Food Pantry leverage World Hunger Day and Feeding America's Hunger Action Month to drive food donations while simultaneously raising awareness about classes, demonstrations, and meal kits available to families in Oneida County.

As part of the business, I wanted to give back to my community but also promote our mission. I had to find a way to help assure that other children in my community did not have to grow up hungry the way I did. As part of our group classes we ask each student to bring two items of nonperishable food that we would then donate to a local faith-based food pantry for those struggling in our community. After each class I take a photo of the group and send it to local media with a press release announcing how much food was donated by the class. It was a good start, but I felt that we could do more to help people who did not know where their next meal was coming from.

World Hunger Day was Sunday, May 28, 2017. In recognition of this day, and because juvenile hunger was a cause near and dear to me, I decided to leverage the opportunity and organize a weeklong food drive.

Budget and Method

We had $0 for our budget. Our method included the following:

- Contacted, pitched the idea, and partnered with local food-related business with local restaurant contacts and donation box delivery resources.
- Acquired cardboard boxes from local department stores.
- Worked with delivery service to distribute and place boxes in strategic locations throughout the county.
- Highlighted and promoted each food drop-off spot via social and traditional media.
- Asked delivery service to provide discounts to customers who donated food and pick up food donations for anyone who could not get to a deposit location.

Goals

We had three primary goals:

1. Collect 200 pounds of nonperishable food during the month of May (a combination of food items and monetary donations). One dollar equals one food item.Enlist five to ten local business partners to facilitate food donations.
2. Partner with a local restaurant food delivery service and deploy a dozen collection boxes in strategic restaurant locations throughout the community for one week.
3. Secure three to five media placements with local TV, radio, print and online media outlets.

To facilitate donations and campaign awareness, I issued a pre-event press release to over 40 local media contacts, and arranged for two morning show radio interviews, a print newspaper brief, and a taped TV interview on the six o'clock news broadcast on the local ABC news affiliate. We used our respective social media channels to raise awareness of the hunger problem in our area and secure food donations. Toward the end of the week I sent a media advisory to all media contacts with the time and day of a photo opportunity of presentation of all donations to the food pantry. While no members of the media attended, we took the opportunity to create broadcast Facebook live videos of the event and took many photos, which were subsequently posted. Additionally, I emailed a post event press release announcing the results with a photo, which was printed in the Utica *Observer Dispatch* daily publication. In all communications, I highlighted my own story of being a hungry child and asked that people help make a difference in the lives of children in our local schools.

The timeline for the campaign was May 15 to May 29, 2017.

Successes

Our successes for the campaign were as follows:

- 12 local restaurants participated in the week-long food collection campaign.
- A local TV news station aired an interview with myself, the other business owner, and an official with the food pantry.
- At the end of the week we were able to raise the profile of our two businesses, awareness about the hunger issue locally, and provide the food pantry with much needed supplies.
- Two weeks after the campaign ended, the local daily newspaper printed a photo of the food collected and people involved with a results-oriented caption.

Failures

At the end of two weeks we came up a short of our goal of 200 pounds of food, with only 186 pounds of nonperishable food for the pantry and its clients.

Next Steps

The media campaign we employed did not work as well as we had hoped, so with the next campaign we took a different approach. The first campaign did not meet its objectives, so as a PR professional I made adjustments in tactics to a less media focused effort and a more grassroots angle. The second campaign was more successful.

Second Campaign: Hunger Action Month: September 1–30

Again, we had $0 for our budget. The timeline for this campaign was August 14th–October 6th, 2017.

Goals

Help St. Margaret's Food Pantry raise 1,500 more pounds of food donations in September, just a few months after asking everyone I knew to donate whatever they could.

Method

I used the mission, recognition, and brand awareness of our cooking school to cold-call local hospitals and large employers and ask for help. I asked my fellow PR colleagues with St. Elizabeth's Hospital, Faxton/St. Luke's Hospital, Empire Blue Cross/Blue Shield Insurance Company, Utica National Insurance, and others to work with their employees to conduct internal food drives for a week or two at a time throughout the month.

Reasoning

Rather than a redundant media campaign, I felt that recruiting influencers with large local employers to organize employees to drive donations would be the most effective tool for a long-term campaign. Following this outreach, I concentrated my efforts on delivering boxes and developing internal communications tools such as promotional signage, email and intranet messaging, social media content, and facts and statistics in an effort to educate and motivate employees to donate food items.

Successes

Our successes for the second campaign are as follows: Ten local business and healthcare partners were recruited to collect food via employee efforts.

- Nine organizations donated at least one full box of food items.
- Between the efforts of the local church that houses the food pantry and our campaign, we raised combined total of over 1,600 pounds of food.

Results

The second campaign was more successful than the first because employees in large companies already participated in volunteer committees that organized various activities to benefit local agencies. Therefore, it was just a matter of contacting the human resources department and identifying the chairperson of the community relations department, asking them to request that employees bring in food over the course of a week or two, and providing them with boxes, signs, and email message templates with statistics about local hunger issues to make the campaign as easy to implement as possible. It did not hurt that employees sometimes feel a little obligated to participate in employer-sanctioned events, especially when it is for a good cause.

Part III: Thoughts to Leave You With

There is not much I would change in my career if given a chance, but there are things I am going to change in the future. I am looking forward to passing down my love for cooking to grandchildren and someday going back to school: culinary school! I want to learn more about food and ways to raise more of it for struggling, hungry families in the world. I envision cooking or teaching culinary skills in my retirement while writing cookbooks, and utilizing my PR skills and experience to continue our mission of educating families and supporting the hungry. And by doing such I won't work one single day, right Dad? The one regret I have from the day I started my first restaurant job to today is that I wish I had listened to my father more and acted on his advice in the moment instead of years later. I wish I had known that he was going to be right about a great many things.

The break that started my career in PR was a volunteer opportunity. I got involved with a club centered around my love and passion for running. I was combining two passions at one time and making a difference in my community. If you are a student, or are just getting started in PR, and want to gain valuable experience, volunteer with nonprofit organizations with causes that are important to you and offer to help them with their PR, marketing, and promotional needs. Nonprofits are always looking for great ideas and people to implement them to raise awareness, increase event participation, and raise funds.

When you get a job in PR (or for that matter just as a practice in life), know your value, always give an honest answer, never be afraid to say, "I don't know but I will find out." In addition, always give accurate information, never miss a deadline, always be a resource, be a problem-solver and not a problem-starter, love your work, be firm with goals but flexible with strategies, continue to learn, and *never* drink with reporters. Remember, as a public relations professional, it isn't always about memorizing everything there is to know about a product, service, or organization but rather establishing relationships with departments or colleagues to be able to put your hands on the needed information at a moment's notice. I have come a long way, learned a great deal, and have had many experiences, but I could not have done any of it without help from family and many friends and colleagues. Let me end this chapter with what has come to be the most important thing my father ever said to me and something I tell my own child almost every day: "Just do what you say you will do and everything else will take care of itself."

Jack Pflanz
Dad/Owner/Operator/Chief Dishwasher
Jack and Mo Cooking Show
https://www.facebook.com/JackandMoCookingShow/notifications/
www.JackandMoCookingShow.com

7 GOVERNMENT PUBLIC RELATIONS

Arlene Guzman

Arlene Guzman is a versatile communications leader who specializes in strategizing and executing campaigns. Arlene brings 15 years of experience working with high-profile clients to tell their stories and effectively manage their public relations and government affairs priorities. She has partnered with both leading and emerging brands in the energy innovation, venture capital, cannabis and nonprofit sectors to create high-impact strategies that result in coverage by top-tier media outlets. Earlier in her career, Arlene worked on the campaigns of notable US Senate and Presidential candidates. She received her master's degree in strategic public relations from George Washington University.

Part I: Personal

I received a Bachelor of Arts degree in Spanish Literary and Cultural Studies from Occidental College in Los Angeles, California. As an undergraduate student I made it a point to gain experience by participating in campus clubs and organizations and through internship opportunities. I interned for the California Republican Party's state headquarters, where I gained knowledge on running local and state-level political campaigns. At Merrill Lynch I became exposed to wealth management and investment practices, and by working for Los Angeles District Attorney Phil Wojdak, I gained first-hand knowledge of the legal system. These internship experiences exposed me to many fields and allowed me to eliminate certain industries as potential career options.

As graduation day approached, I was filled with excitement and fear: excitement, because I would be the first in my family to graduate from college; fear, because I did not know what type of career I would pursue post-graduation. At 21 and 22 years of age, many of my classmates had decided on their careers and had their next steps decided. Many of the science majors would go on to medical or dental school, the business and economics majors would head to consulting or investment firms, and many of the political science majors were law school–bound. I was unsure of what the future had in store for me, which was unsettling. In the days following graduation I reflected on what elements my ideal job description would entail and narrowed in on event planning, networking, writing, and marketing. I searched for these job descriptions on career search sites such as indeed.com, craigslist.com, monster.com, and LinkedIn.com and eventually found a position at the University of Southern California's Marshall School of Business alumni affairs office, and it was there where I would proceed to kick off my communications career.

After my time as an assistant director of alumni affairs at the Marshall School of Business, I was recruited for an opportunity at the California Governor and First Lady's Conference on Women, also known as The Women's Conference, an organization that was led by then California First Lady Maria Shriver. During my time at the Women's Conference I primarily worked on the organization's branding efforts and developed partnership opportunities with more than fifty Fortune 500 companies. Most notably, during my time there I had the unique opportunity to collaborate with several leading public relations and public affairs agencies in a client role capacity. As their client, I learned about managing client expectations and internal politics, strategic planning, the importance of a quality work product, and the significance of hiring people for their business expertise. Through this experience, I was able to gain several best practices that I would later apply to my own public relations work.

Following the Women's Conference, I took a position as the marketing, communications, and government relations specialist at VantagePoint Capital Partners, a Silicon Valley-based firm that at the time, invested in energy efficiency and innovation, information technology, and healthcare. In this capacity, I worked directly with the chief operating officer to develop and deploy public relations strategies, branding campaigns, and media relations opportunities for the firm, the firm leadership, and for 60-plus portfolio companies. The portfolio companies were companies that our firm had invested in, and they varied in size and maturity. In my role, I provided communications and public relations operational resources in a similar capacity as what a public relations agency would have provided them. Other responsibilities included developing budgets for department projects; managing external vendors (public relations agencies, media monitoring services, independent contractors, etc.); developing relationships with members of the press; and investor relations, which included the production of the investor annual meeting. The work was exciting and intellectually stimulating.

As the youngest member of the VantagePoint staff, and one of the few women at the firm, I focused on establishing credibility by avoiding office politics, making sound and well researched recommendations, identifying proof points to support recommendations, and, most importantly, forcing myself to ask for help when it was needed. As you begin your career, always remember to ask questions and for additional explanations in order to make sure that you understand what is required of you. In my current role, I have the opportunity to work with and supervise many recent college grads. A recurring theme among this demographic is that younger employees do not ask enough questions about work direction or work product. Asking questions will allow you to be fully informed about expectations, which will allow you to produce the best work possible. Regularly asking questions will also allow others to form positive impressions of you. By asking questions you will come across as invested in the company, detail-oriented, and committed to delivering good work.

After nearly four years at VantagePoint, I moved to the East Coast and began a public relations practice in Raleigh, North Carolina. At the time, job options in the region were extremely limited, so I started my practice as a sole proprietor and partnered with several start-up companies, business membership organizations, government, and nonprofit projects. Most of my clients came largely through referrals from prior clients, former colleagues, and through networking. Each client had unique communications needs that required branding, media relations, and digital strategy expertise. Having my own practice allowed me to have a flexible schedule, work remotely, and be my own boss. As a small business owner, I worked from a home office which was nice most of the time, although at times, not being in an office at times left me craving human interaction and a team dynamic. During this time I decided to pursue a master's degree in strategic public relations from the George Washington School of Political Management. The academic setting of my graduate school program proved to be a great antidote for the isolation I was experiencing in my professional setting.

After two and a half years, a West Coast relocation took place. Armed with a new master's degree, I put my consulting practice on hold and decided to pursue a more traditional work environment. I took a position as associate vice president at a national public relations firm that works primarily with clients in the higher education and real estate sectors, and with local government agencies. In my role, I managed staff and led the strategy and execution for the various accounts I worked on. Overall, agency life tends to be very busy. From my experience, people who do well in agency settings are typically great multitaskers, have good interpersonal skills, work well under pressure, are excellent public speakers, enjoy networking, and are above-average writers who have command of grammar, tone, and AP style.

An important lesson learned through my agency experience—and something you may want to consider for any future agency or in-house job you might hold—is that there is typically not a right or wrong way to do things. Really, for example, as long as the important details are present, there really isn't a right or wrong way to format a press release or plan an event. Instead, your key to success will depend on your ability to learn to adapt your work to fulfill your bosses' and company's stylistic preferences. Whenever possible you should make it a point to ask for sample documents, explicitly asking what you should leave out or avoid, and asking for peer feedback from other employees. The sooner you can learn and master these stylistic preferences, the more successful you will be in your role.

Part II: Professional Public Affairs and Government Relations Case Study: Drive the Dream

Public affairs and government relations are functions of public relations that are critical to an organization's effectiveness. Public affairs and government relations work is applied to issues that concern the public directly. This type of work is typically related to government legislation and policy.

In September 2013, the California Plug-In Electric Vehicle Collaborative produced Drive the Dream, a government relations campaign that brought together Governor Edmund "Jerry" G. Brown Jr. and more than 40 Fortune 500 CEOs to announce corporate commitments aimed at expanding the plug-in electric vehicle (PEV) market exponentially throughout California. The public outreach event would target leaders and decision-makers from the private sector to participate in a roundtable discussion and press conference event with Governor Brown. As explained in the following section, Drive the Dream is an example of how public (government) and private (corporate) sector partnerships can contribute to furthering government agendas and corporate initiatives alike.

About the California Plug-In Electric Vehicle Collaborative

The California Plug-In Electric Vehicle Collaborative was a public/private Sacramento-based organization, comprised of 47 members who partnered to work together to move the plug-in electric vehicle market in California. The Collaborative members consisted of automakers, utility companies, electric vehicle charging equipment and network providers, elected and appointed government officials, environmental organizations, and research institutions. In 2007, the California Plug-In Electric Vehicle Collaborative closed shop and a new California-based nonprofit, Veloz, opened its place. Veloz is continuing the work of The Collaborative by working to get people excited about electric cars.

As stated on the Collaborative website (http://www.pevcollaborative.org), the organization was established to achieve six goals for PEV market success in California by 2020. The goals were:

- That consumers' experiences with PEVs were positive.
- Ownership costs of PEVs were competitive with conventional vehicles.
- PEV charging integrates smoothly into an increasingly clean, efficient, reliable, and safe electricity grid.
- PEVs advance energy security, air quality, climate change, and public health goals.
- The PEV market helps create jobs and directly benefited California's economy.
- The PEV market moves beyond early adopters to mainstream consumers.

California's Commitment to Plug-In Electric Vehicles

The Collaborative goals were developed to support Governor Brown's strategy to reduce the state's greenhouse gas emissions by 40 percent (below the 1990 levels) before 2030. This was directed in California Executive Order B-30-15.[1] California is the nation's largest market for cars and light-duty trucks, and the state's transportation sector accounted for approximately 37 percent of the state's overall greenhouse emissions.[2] As such, the transportation sector, and specifically the migrating of California's transportation system away from gasoline-powered vehicles and toward zero-emission vehicles, provided an exciting opportunity to make progress toward achieving the state goals.

On March 23, 2012, Governor Brown issued Executive Order B-16-2012 to "encourage the development and success of zero-emission vehicles to protect the environment, stimulate economic growth and improve the quality of life in the State."[3] The order also decreed that the California Air Resources Board, the California Energy Commission, the Public Utilities Commission, and other relevant state agencies work with the Plug-in Electric Vehicle Collaborative and the California Fuel Cell Partnership to establish various benchmarks by 2015. These benchmarks included:

- The State's major metropolitan areas would have capabilities to accommodate zero-emission vehicles, each with infrastructure plans and a streamlined permitting process;
- The State's manufacturing sector would expand zero-emission vehicle and component manufacturing;
- The private sector's investment in zero-emission vehicle infrastructure would grow; and
- The State's academic and research institutions would contribute to zero-emission vehicle research, innovation, and education.

Partnering with the California Plug-in Electric Vehicle Collaborative

On April 25, 2013, the California Plug-in Electric Vehicle Collaborative issued a request for proposal (RFP) for work on a Governor's CEO Roundtable on Electric Transportation: Workplace Charging and Plug-in Electric Vehicle Purchases. The Collaborative, in partnership with several state agencies including

---

1. See http://www.energy.ca.gov/renewables/tracking_progress/documents/electric_vehicle.pdf

2. California Air Resources Board, GHG Emission Inventory 2016 Edition, http://www.arb.ca.gov/cc/inventory/data/data.htm

3. Executive Order B-16-2012; https://www.gov.ca.gov/news.php?id=17472

the Bay Area Air Quality Management District, the South Coast Air Quality Management District, CALSTART, and other stakeholders, had previously been awarded a grant from the US Department of Energy (DOE) for Implementation Initiatives to Advance Alternative Fuel Markets. The RFP solicited formal proposals from individuals and organizations that would, under contract with the Collaborative, organize a Governor's CEO roundtable event. Under the RFP, the selected vendor would secure the venue for the event, and ensure participation by both the Governor of California and CEOs from the State's largest employers. The US Department of Energy (DOE) for Implementation Initiatives to Advance Alternative Fuel Markets grant allocated a budget not to exceed $81,000 for the campaign.[4]

According to the the RFP, the Collaborative and the California Governor's Office would host the Governor's CEO roundtable and press conference event. A roundtable is also commonly known as an interactive meeting. The intention of the roundtable was to influence California business executives to make commitments that would help the state meet its electric vehicle goals. At the roundtable, Governor Brown would describe California's leadership and vision for rapid deployment of PEVs throughout the state, and business executives would be encouraged to announce quantitative commitments and timelines for PEV purchases and infrastructure changes. Specifically, the corporate executives would be asked to commit to:

1. Increasing the number of plug-in electric vehicles in their corporate fleets;
2. Installing electric vehicle chargers for employees and customers; and
3. Creating employee incentive programs to offset the purchase of plug-in electric vehicles.

For the RFP, Cathie Bennett Warner from the CBW Group, Tamara Gould from Waking State Design, and I partnered and submitted a reply to RFP under the CBW Group name. On May 22, 2013, the CBW Group was selected to organize the Governor's CEO Roundtable on Electric Vehicles. As the chosen contractor, my team, in close coordination with Collaborative staff, would help the PEV Collaborative identify and secure CEO commitments to purchase PEVs, install workplace charging stations, and create employee incentives programs, in addition to securing a venue location for the roundtable in the San Francisco Bay Area. In addition, our team would be responsible for managing the event planning and logistics, as well as managing the public and media outreach efforts. Three of us from the CBW Group started our work immediately.

---

4. See http://www.pevcollaborative.org/sites/all/themes/pev/files/RFP_GO_CEO_Roundtable_130425_FINAL.pdf

Project Tasks

The California Plug-in Electric Vehicle Collaborative RFP specified a list of tasks required for the development and execution of the governor's CEO roundtable. Our team had four months to plan the event, ending with the event on September 16, 2013 at the Exploratorium in San Francisco. Details surrounding the approach for each task are described in the following sections.

Task 1: Identify and Recruit California CEOs

We started our CEO recruiting process by first identifying California's top 200 employers. Initial CEO invitations and outreach was conducted via email. The first round of emails were submitted to government relations executives. From there, we held follow-up phone calls with key corporate stakeholders to discuss the campaign that would ultimately be named, "Drive the Dream". During our outreach the team would ask the stakeholders to commit to the three electric vehicles goals stated in the previous section (increasing the number of vehicles and chargers, and establishing an incentive plan). Overall, we pitched over 100 companies to make commitments to Drive the Dream. In the end, 40 corporations made commitments to electric vehicles and attended the roundtable and press conference event.

Task 2: Plan and Execute Roundtable Logistics

Our team took a less-is-more approach in designing the Drive the Dream event. We followed the following steps to ensure success:

- Drafted the event program and run of show in consultation with the client;
- Booked program participants, managed their role, and finalized scripts and talking points for participating speakers;
- Designed the overall look and feel of the event through branding and graphic design;
- Staged impactful visuals for media coverage;
- Planned and budgeted for refreshments and food service; and
- Planned and budgeted for AV requirements and other technical onsite issues.

The most critical component of a successful event is the venue. Although it is often said that you shouldn't judge a book by its cover, the venue provides the first impression for any event and can inspire attendees, make for a beautiful backdrop and set the tone for the event. We ultimately decided on the Exploratorium, which bills itself as a "public learning laboratory exploring the world through science, art, and human perception." The Exploratorium's mission, combined with the San Francisco bay as a backdrop, was a reminder of the beauty of nature, and provided an impactful visual backdrop for attendees and the media. In addition, our team convinced the Exploratorium to waive their $35,000 event rental fee, which allowed us to keep the event within the budget. The fee reduction and hosting Drive the Dream at the Exploratorium was mutually beneficial: the media coverage surrounding Drive the Dream brought positive exposure for the facility.

Task 3: Develop, Distribute, and Execute Media Relations Campaign

Our immediate media relations efforts consisted of message development and pro-active media outreach efforts which started in June, three months prior to the event.

MESSAGING

Our team was tasked with developing the roundtable messages to be used in materials, speeches, and in communication with the press and media. We developed a message playbook that was segmented by audience. The message playbook included:

- An umbrella message and overarching event vision statement;
- Development of boilerplate for the event;
- Talking points, anecdotes, and sound bites;
- Q&A for difficult and most frequent issues; and
- Messages segmented by audience for corporations, elected officials, environmentalists, and auto industry influencers.

MEDIA OUTREACH

Our team drafted and released a series of media advisories, press releases, and social media posts to garner media interest around Drive the Dream. The media outreach goal was to garner statewide coverage on the campaign through traditional media and social media outlet events, and on the commitments made by California-based corporations. The media outreach efforts took place as follows:

- June 24, 2013: Preliminary press discussions outreach to reporters announcing Drive the Dream begins.
- July 16, 2013: Twitter account @PEVDreams became active (the account is now closed).
- August 9, 2013: A press release announcing the Drive the Dream event was released. August 29 – September 15, 2013: Targeted media outreach was conducted, including mass group outreach (via constant contact mailings) and personal outreach which was done through phone calls, emails and direct tweets to reporters.
- September 16, 2013: Governor Brown's office distributed a press release announcing Drive the ream and other Bay Area events. In addition, several participating corporations issued their individual press releases announcing their corporate commitments to plug-in electric vehicles.

FIGURE 7.1 Drive the Dream Logo.

Task 4: Create Ancillary Events

We added a luncheon to the larger Drive the Dream event and secured former Secretary of State George Shultz and producer, director, and winemaker Francis Ford Coppola, both enthusiastic electric vehicle owners, to participate and speak at the event. In total, nearly 300 people attended various parts of the event.

Task 5: Create, Design, and Production of Event Collateral

This task include marketing, print materials, the agenda, invitations, and event packets. As with any branding exercise, there were several iterations of the logo, tagline, and name design. The two name and tagline finalists were: Drive the Dream: Committing to PEVs for All; and California Driving Change: Amping up the PEV Market. We ultimately decided on Drive the Dream.

As part of the brand selection process, the logos and tagline options were vetted by automotive industry leaders, government leaders, marketing and brand experts, and the client. The final brand elements were used on all event-related emails, website, and day-of signage.

To stay on theme with the environmental message, all communiques, invitations, and registrations efforts were done digitally via the Drive the Dream website.

Task 6: Planning Meetings, Progress Reports, and Post-Event Report

Meetings with the California Plug-in Electric Vehicle Collaborative team took place every other week. Our internal team had a weekly planning meeting along, with many impromptu calls, emails and in-person meetings.

Since the project had an ambitious timeline, we shared real-time project updates including corporate commitments via a Dropbox folder and email. The post-event report was compiled to highlight the project outcomes to the client and key stakeholders.

Task 7: Proposed Budget and Timeline
BUDGET

An overall budget of $81,000 was outlined in the RFP. The budgeted amount would pay our team's consulting fees for producing the event, and all hard costs (rentals, materials, and supplies) associated with the governor's roundtable. Considering that the event was expected to take place in the San Francisco Bay Area, a costly part of the country, the budgeted amount was considered relatively small for an event of this caliber.

In order to cover the costs associated with executing task 4, our team solicited sponsorships from roundtable participants. BMW, Nissan, Coca Cola, and GM made financial commitments that helped offset the cost of the luncheon. By sponsoring the luncheon, these corporations gained increased visibility by being listed as official sponsors of the Drive the Dream campaign.

PROJECT TIMELINE

The project timeline was largely driven by the venue availability. From start to finish, the project planning and execution took approximately four months. Details included:

- **Month 1 focus: exploratory stage with the California Plug-In Electric Vehicle Collaborative and key stakeholders to identify clear goals and develop campaign messaging.** During the first month of the project, we planned to discuss process of inviting and securing participants and venue selection. This included locking down Governor Brown and key attendees' availability. Next, we began development of our CEO target guest list. By the end of the month, we also identified brand identity and distributed save-the-date invitations. During this time, we also planned to develop event webpage and registration site.
- **Months 2–3 focus: venue and vendors secured.** The top priority of the second month was to secure the location. In July, the venue and all vendor contracts were executed. The remainder of this time we continued the CEO outreach and increased our focus on social media channels to promote the Collaborative, the event, and participating corporations.
- **Month 4 focus: finalize CEO attendance, run-of-show, and media attendance.** During the final month our team prepared press kits (virtual and paper), ordered printed collateral, and executed day-of logistics.

Drive the Dream Results

Overwhelmingly, Drive the Dream was considered a success by the Collaborative, participants, and the CBW Group. Campaign highlights include:

- In Governor Brown's remarks before an audience of more than 150 guests, he celebrated the variety of PEVs on display and announced that he would sign important legislation for PEV rebates and incentives to ensure their success in the marketplace.

FIGURE 7.2 Governor Brown Addressing Drive The Dream.

- The event highlighted 40 California businesses including the Coca-Cola Company, Google, and Walgreens, whose executives announced substantial investments in new workplace charging for PEVs, corporate fleet purchases, and increased employee PEV purchases.
- Total number of corporate commitments to increase the number of plug-in electric vehicles in their corporate fleets: 1,509.
- Total number of corporate commitments to increase the number of electric vehicle chargers for employees and customers: 2,033.
- The #DRIVETHEDREAM hashtag reached over 313,000 Twitter accounts.
- 18 media and press outlets registered at Drive the Dream, including Bloomberg News, CBS Radio, Fast Company, KQED, the San Francisco Chronicle, and others.

Part III: Tips for Consideration

If I were given the opportunity to restart my public relations career, I would focus on finding work in one industry that inspired me personally and professionally. In general, public relations skills are transferable to any industry, which can be both a blessing and a curse. On the one hand, once you master public relations strategy and execution skills, and you can excel as a public relations practitioner in any industry. On the other hand, as a young PR practitioner it might be difficult to find the perfect industry to kick-start your career in, simply because you may not know what industry you're truly passionate about. Even if you do know what you want to do, it is possible that the industry you are interested in poses geographic limitations. For example, venture capital roles have historically been abundant in the San Francisco Bay Area, New York, Los Angeles, and Boston and not so much in middle America. Or perhaps you are so worried about forthcoming student loan payments that you are desperate to take any job in the field. Regardless of your drivers, I would encourage all people new to the industry to identify an area you love and work hard to find an opportunity in it. Learning about an industry and making industry contacts takes time, so get invested in the industry you're in. For me, working in government affairs in PR roles combined my passions from college with my corporate experience in a way that made me feel like I was using my skills to promote causes that I am passionate about, such as education, women's issues, and the environment.

My professional experiences have allowed me to work in the nonprofit, venture capital, technology, entertainment, education, and real estate sectors. I have enjoyed working in certain sectors more than others, and think this was reflected in the quality of my work. The more you enjoy your work, the better your work product tends to be. While I always bring my strategic public relations knowledge and experience to each new opportunity, each industry change came with a significant learning curve. In order to be successful, I had to learn each industry's unique audience demographics and public relations sensitives. As applicable, I had to familiarize myself on the leading trade shows and industry events and leading publications. Most importantly, I needed to identify and build relationships with industry reporters, an activity that takes a significant amount of time and effort, which would have been avoided if I had committed to developing a practice in one specific industry.

Form my experience, I have learned and witnessed that the best public relations practitioners are voracious media consumers. Regularly reading, watching, or listening to media allows you to develop industry best practices, keep abreast of emerging trends, gain familiarity with reporters and influencers who cover your industry, benchmark competitor efforts, and learn what issues and topics are relevant to your target audiences. In short, the more media you consume, the more successful you will be in your role as a communications professional.

Reading trade publications such as *PRWeek Magazine*, *PR Daily*, *PR News*, *O'Dwyer's*, *BizBash*, and *Adweek* may help you gain new public relations skills. By reading about award-winning campaigns and new technologies, you may be inspired to implement these tactics into your own public relations campaigns.

Along with being avid media consumers, it is important that you make professional growth and development a priority at all stages of your career. Professional development opportunities include (but are not limited to) attending conferences and trade organization events, including those hosted by the Public Relations Society of America; listening to vlogs and podcasts; or enrolling in a class at a local college or university. A growing list of employers offer tuition reimbursement benefits, which can help offset the cost of professional development opportunities. You should plan to use these benefits and actively seeking opportunities that allow you to expand your network and your skill set, which will ultimately make you a more marketable employee and future candidate.

Throughout your career you should strive to establish professional credibility and expertise beyond your company walls. An easy and cost-effective way to do this is by populating digital channels such as a personal blog, LinkedIn profile, or other social media channel. By using these platforms, you will be able to share your professional accomplishments, project experience, and highlight insights and perspective on industry issues and trends. Establishing this professional credibility will help make you a more marketable employee, which may help with your overall career progression and success.

My final advice is: find a mentor. An area of professional development that should never be taken for granted is mentorship. Mentors can be some of the most inspiring people who you interact and work with on a regular basis. These people will get to know you and how you think, act, and contribute to an organization, and can help advocate on your behalf. Ideally, these individuals are several steps ahead of you in your field or industry. Mentors can help you navigate the industry and provide meaningful insights and relationships that can help you throughout your career. My mentors have been especially helpful in helping win new business, negotiate pay, and when brainstorming career moves.

Arlene Guzman
Communications Strategist
LinkedIn: https://www.linkedin.com/in/arlene/

PUBLIC AFFAIRS IN PUBLIC RELATIONS

Nicole Kuklok-Waldman

Nicole Kuklok-Waldman is a founding partner of ColLAborate, a public affairs firm she owns with her two business partners, Katherine Hennigan Ohanesian and Tracey Chavira. At ColLAborate, Nicole advocates for businesses to ensure the best results for her clients. From regulatory challenges to development projects, Nicole specializes in a comprehensive advocacy approach and is known for integrating community outreach, communication with elected officials and community leaders, and honesty backed up by evidentiary support to ensure a positive and desired result.

In addition to ColLAborate, Nicole teaches at the University of Southern California as adjunct faculty, is involved with several nonprofits, and is a leader with Rodan and Fields in Los Angeles. Prior to founding ColLAborate, Nicole practiced land-use law at major law firms in Los Angeles. She currently lives in the San Fernando Valley area of Los Angeles with her husband, Stuart Waldman, two children, and two rescue dogs.

Part I: Personal

My career really began, like most law students, in my second year of law school. Traditionally, law students interview for their law firm positions in the beginning of their second year of law school. They then "summer" at a law firm, and, if it goes well, they receive an offer to work at the firm after their third year of law school and after taking the bar exam. I interviewed at several firms and accepted a position at a popular firm in Los Angeles at the time, Brobeck. However, during my third year of law school the firm dissolved, and by then all the jobs around the city were taken by law students who had summered at other firms. I got lucky and was able to obtain a position at another large law firm in Los Angeles after I graduated, but did not get to select my preferred practice area. After a year and a half of work I did not enjoy, I was prepared to give up practicing law, but decided to apply for some positions that I thought would be compatible with my political interests and with the events I regularly attended with my husband, who at the time was the chief of staff for a California state legislator.

In Los Angeles the most political area of law is generally land use, which addresses the potential increase in value of land through approval of zoning changes. After applying for several positions, I ended up being hired by a large Los Angeles law firm, Latham and Watkins, that had a thriving land-use practice. I learned a great deal there, and worked a lot—at least 2,400 hours of billable time, annually—not including time devoted to work lunches, evening events, and other time consuming but career-building activities and firm obligations. Through a series of choices, including a desire to have a better work–life balance as well as the market crash of 2008, I ended up working at a boutique law firm with several partners from my larger firm, Armbruster, Goldsmith & Delvac, and worked there for several years.

Land use and development is a male-dominated industry. As with most client-service industries, you are expected to build a book of business over time as you become more senior, so technical expertise and competence is not the only skill required to be successful. After more than ten years practicing land use, I had become a solid technician. However, when it came to having a book of business of my own, the work tended to go other ways, generally to my male superiors, who either kept that work (and related business development credit) for themselves, or gave it to those with whom they associated most closely. In addition, my husband and I had decided to start a family, and with that came my desire to have more flexibility in my time and also consider how I was converting each hour worked into money, and how I wanted to better leverage my time. Around that time I was offered an opportunity at Cerrell Associates, a public relations firm with a lobbying practice. While I would not need as much of the technical skill that was required of me as a lawyer at that firm, I could use my technical skills as an add-value opportunity and could focus more of my business development on relationship-building. As a woman, it seemed that clients were more inclined to take me seriously as a relationship-builder than as a technician, despite my skills.

For point of reference, the public relations subset of public affairs and government affairs relates primarily to communications with elected officials and communications with constituents of elected officials on behalf of a client. A public affairs firm acts as an advocate on behalf of clients through direct communication with elected officials, government staffs, and government departments, which is often called "lobbying"; engages in coalition-building, which is bringing key groups together around shared interests to advocate for action by elected officials; and coordinates communication with stakeholders on behalf of a client for the benefit of an elected official, oftentimes referred to as community outreach.

Joining Cerrell Associates and my change to the public relations industry enabled me to do a couple of things. For starters, it allowed me to learn how smaller businesses operate, and how they cross-sell. It also allowed me to finesse my product offerings to be more amenable to women in my industry. While bringing in clients as a lawyer had proven difficult, bringing in clients in the public relations and affairs arena, especially given my extensive education and legal background, proved easier.

The firm also provided me, in the short term, with a mentor. The firm's president at the time, Lisa Gritzner, helped me navigate the sometimes bumpy transition from law to public affairs. A year after I joined the firm, however, Lisa left, and it became clear it was time for me to move forward. I later started my own firm with two former employees of Cerrell Associates, and we created our woman-owned firm, Collaborate.

This choice to go out on my own once again opened the doors for me to do a number of things I had been unable to do when employed by others. At the outset, owning my own firm enabled me to choose my own clients and coworkers. It also empowered me to run a business on my own time, which was something I had been increasingly craving due to my two small children. I also appreciated the opportunity to work remotely more often, eliminating much of my regular commuting time. It hasn't always been a flawless journey; I essentially changed careers in my mid-thirties. But now that I am living my dream, I wouldn't have it any other way.

There have been many surprises in my career trajectory that I think can be illustrative as you consider your own career path, some of which I could plan for, others that came as a surprise. Of course, this list relates primarily to my experience, and your experience may vary. Each of these learnings is discussed in turn.

First, a career as a woman is different than your career would be if you were a man. I am not trying to be discouraging, but I am trying to adjust expectations about how things may progress. I naively believed, in my twenties, that my excellent performance would ensure that I had the same opportunities as my male counterparts, and on paper, that continues to be true. But as long as relationships and not actual, quantitative tools determine success, the majority of men in most professional settings will continue to favor men, either outwardly or inwardly. This can take many forms—it can be discussion of deals after work when friends all go and socialize with each other, or can be when you are told you don't share priorities because part of the family workload falls to you instead of a stay-at-home spouse. This sexism can also be that some bad actor in the past colored management's characterization of all of a certain class—never overtly, of course. While many of the institutional barriers at most organizations are gone, it is the social barriers that will continue to favor those already in the higher ranks.

As a woman, you can address this disparity one of two ways. You can either continue to try and push forward through institutions, acting as though the barriers don't exist, or you can acknowledge those barriers and try to strategically use those barriers to get what you want. I would suggest you consider the latter. To that end, I would get an accurate lay of the land at any organization and establish how you are going to use the existing structure to position yourself for success. Who needs to see you working hard? Who do you need to become friends with? Who makes the real power decisions in your organization, and whose voice is heard? How are you going to map out getting what you want in any institution? Who is going to help you manage the business structure and advocate on your behalf?

I believe the largest gap in my career has been my lack of a mentor. This is a tricky issue. An assigned mentor through a program is not necessarily a true mentor. A mentor is a person who will meet with you, who will give you strategic advice, and who will affirmatively go out of their way to help you. A mentor is a person who will make a call on your behalf and for no one else. A mentor is a person who will give you honest feedback, even when it is negative. And don't mistake a friend, coworker, or supervisor for a mentor; that can seriously derail your journey. A mentor is not just a cheerleader, he or she is someone who will go out for you on your behalf, who will gun for you. If you can find that person, good for you. But keep looking and don't give up if you haven't yet found that person. And in the meantime, do your best to be that person to others. It is your professional duty.

The third most important observation I can offer you is to consider the whole of your life, and not just your job, when attempting to set goals and plan your career. Consider how everything will fit together. One of the biggest mistakes I made when structuring my career and plans was to try to path my career without consideration for things I loved and wanted in my life. I thought if I got the career in order, everything else would fall into line. Contrary to that assumption, I learned that you are the captain of this ship and you need to set boundaries for yourself because no one else will.

For example, if you love to travel to remote places, maybe a career path that requires you to be accessible 24/7 isn't the best strategy moving forward. If you want to get married and have children, how are you going to date when you are in the office until 11 p.m. every night? How are you going to care for children if your career requires constant travel? If you want a dog and work unpredictable hours, who will feed and walk the dog when something comes up? Take a good look at the lives of those 10 or more years ahead of you in your career. What do their lives look like, and who shares your priorities? Who has a quality of life that you want? Use those observations as a model to establish how you can structure your path to do the same.

I also think it is important to consider how careers have changed in the last thirty years. My father worked for a total of two firms while I was growing up. I have already worked for several, and that is the new norm. I also wear several hats—lawyer, consultant, professor, board member, and CEO. How is the market changing, and how are you going to be ready for that change when it occurs? Consider how the life of the 20-year career taxi driver was changed with Lyft, or how sales careers have changed with the Internet. You have to prepare for change and be flexible to secure your future.

When I went to law school, I thought I would work at a large law firm for my entire career. That business model has changed, as has my perspective on what matters to me. Over time, consider building flexibility and additional streams of income into your career plans. This can include aggressive retirement savings to give yourself flexibility, a side hustle, or crafting for Etsy or hosting on AirBnB. Be ready for change, because it is coming. Nothing lasts forever, and that's O.K. Just do your best to prepare and ensure that you have the best strategy to be responsive to the market and potential changes that might occur.

Lastly, and I cannot emphasize this enough, self-care is key. No one will care for you. No one will force you to take time to meditate, exercise, eat well, or take a mental health day. No one will make you have dinner with friends, prioritize family, or go to yoga or spin class. You must take that initiative yourself. Your body is your best asset in this business, and if it is not functioning or slows down, that endangers your career. I come from a business where lawyers regularly work themselves to death. Lawyers have incredibly high rates for alcoholism and drug addiction, and pay ridiculous amounts for health insurance due to high incidence rates. Work will always be there, and will always be important. You are tasked with setting boundaries for yourself. And while this does not mean you should leave the office at the strike of 5 p.m. every day, it does mean that if you're answering texts on a regular basis at 2 a.m., it is probably time to consider some boundaries.

Part II: Case Study in Public Affairs PR: Junior League of Los Angeles Public Policy Institute

Interestingly, my case study comes not from my actual line of employment, but from my work in the nonprofit leadership sphere working in public affairs PR. The roles that I most enjoy bridge my education, passion, and experience, fitting perfectly in public affiars as it relates primarily to communications with both elected officials and constituents of elected officials on behalf of a client. This also frequently takes the shape of public policy and community outreach.

Throughout my career, I have been on boards of directors for several nonprofits. In the public policy board director role for the Junior League of Los Angeles, I was in charge of a number of programs, including a program I had inherited called the Public Policy Institute. My predecessor had obtained a large grant to create a program intended to train members in skills needed for public policy by placing League members in UCLA Extension Classes. The program was given funding for two years through a related foundation, with the intention that the program would become self-funding after a two-year incubation period.

I reviewed the Public Policy Institute program, and it was very clear that I couldn't figure out how to fund it to move forward. I could not figure out how to sell a program that would, in essence, ask for donations to send college-educated career women in their twenties, thirties, and forties to UCLA. I felt like I had inherited a red herring, and focused on how to make the program survive. I didn't want to have to face the foundation funding the program and tell them it couldn't work without their money.

Through the Junior League I had a new member, called an assistant, to help me as a director. My assistant was an amazing woman named September Hill. We sat down and strategized about how we could save the program. We felt there were a couple key issues: first of all, we had to get the cost of the program down significantly. In order to make the program sustainable, we had to reduce the overall financial cost of the program so that it could be supported within the existing Junior League budget, which was a rough ask. Second, we had to figure out how to get the desired training in-house for next to free, with the net goal of the program being a "program in a box," which would allow the program to replicate long after September and I were around to keep it alive.

September and I developed a curriculum that would use local elected official's staffs and League members to train other members and nonprofits through a series of classes and readings. This would enable the program to use an existing framework year after year, guest speakers in addition to speakers from the Junior League's public policy team, which would allow for expertise to draw outside of the League and would keep costs low. We also created a second component for internships to allow participants who were interested to work with elected officials and nonprofits on legislative activities.

With this new structure, we were able to take the program immediately from three to five students to twelve. With this new size we allowed any active member of the League to join, as well as opening the doors to nonprofit partners and new members of the Junior League, called provisionals. Everyone was clamoring to join the program.

We were able to bring in a number of publicly employed and nonprofit speakers to discuss how to effectively shepherd legislation through the legislative process, how to comply with the law, and how to address best practices. The program was very popular, and our costs were limited to readings and speaker gifts, as our model did not rely on paid speakers. September and I were thrilled, and felt great about what we had created.

Unfortunately, that was not the end of the story. While the program was very popular and had gotten very positive reviews, it still had to be funded in the future, and that required an allocation through the Junior League for future years. This was done in the spring through a Junior League meeting called the project evaluation committee meeting. Like most nonprofits, there is always less funding than there are ideas, and this meeting is where program budgeting was completed and programs were evaluated. I knew the Public Policy Institute program had an issue for a couple of reasons, the key issue being that there was no additional money for any program, and less money for existing programs. I was going to have to fight for the program to get funding.

More pressing, however, was the fact that the president of the Junior League at the time had created her own leadership program. To make matters worse, it was also through a grant from the same foundation. She needed to secure future

Junior League funding for her program at the same time I would need to secure funding for my program. Her program was fundamentally top-heavy and relied on outside consultants, and therefore required significant funding from the League. The president loved her program and wanted to do anything to ensure its survival.

I figured out that the biggest threat to Public Policy Institute was the president's leadership program, formally known as the Leadership Development Institute. After learning that, I sat down, wrote down the names of all the members of the committee, started planning out how to approach each of them on an individual basis. From there I started calling, meeting, and reaching out. Strategically, I didn't contact those who I knew would not be my votes; I secured the votes I knew I would have, and I lobbied the votes I thought I could get. I counted. I met with my Junior League advisor, Susan Steinhauser, and strategized how to reach out to the older organizational members who were lesser known to me at the time.

I also went over how the project evaluation committee meeting would be structured and how the agenda was prepared. This was key. Essentially, the meeting would evaluate each item in its placement on the agenda, while also running a budget. So, for example, if Program A on the agenda was cancelled, the increase to the budget would be added immediately, while if a change to Program B was given additional budget, that would also immediately be calculated, showing the net gain or loss. This enabled the committee to keep a running budget tally.

The president's leadership program was expensive, and would have wiped out any future capacity to budget for my program in the future. So in addition to lobbying my votes, I needed to make sure the Public Policy Institute was on the agenda before the president's leadership program. I couldn't afford to be on the agenda near the end, and absolutely could not be placed on the agenda after the president's leadership program. That would have been fatal. I worked with the member in charge of the agenda to obtain a preferable position on the agenda, ensuring that my program would be considered before the president's leadership program.

The day of the project evaluation committee meeting, I was ready. I had cut my budget, I had lined up my votes, and I had established what drove each individual member of the committee and used it to the program's advantage. I also started to predict what my opponents would do. I figured out that they were driven by certain motivations that they assumed motivated everyone else, too. This was really enlightening. When I sat down and tried to predict my opponent's strategy, I was able to hone in on it because I knew what motivated me: I was trying to save the program and do what I felt was best for the organization, while many others voted simply to agree with their friends. But what I also learned was that they predicted my motivations by what motivated them, not me. As a result, they failed to get outside of themselves strategically.

At the beginning of the meeting, I started hearing about an anonymous donor. Apparently, the president's surrogate on the committee had floated the possibility that an anonymous donor had stepped forward offering to pay half of the cost of the president's leadership program indefinitely. It had become clear to the president that the cost of her program was an issue. While I also knew cost was an issue, I also knew that the bigger issue was agenda placement due to budgeting, because the president's leadership program, even at half price, would still wipe out the possibility for maintaining the Public Policy Institute. At that point, I pushed. I pushed and pushed and pushed, to the point of annoyance and nagging, to get my item heard quickly. I was clear that I wanted my item to be discussed as quickly as possible.

At that point, I had severely annoyed the chair of the meeting and it was my turn; my program was being considered. I gave my presentation, and went through how I had changed the program, how I had reduced costs as much as possible to ensure sustainability, and I presented my budget. It was during this presentation that the president's surrogate on the committee realized what was happening. She realized that approval of my program would almost surely mean death for her friend's program. And she screamed. She seriously screamed. She started shouting that we should consider all of the foundation-granted programs at the same time. The committee chair told her we would consider her program next. But it was too late. I had gotten in ahead, I had the votes, and my program was approved.

I was ecstatic. Even better, September Hill and I submitted an application to the Association of Junior Leagues International for an award for the program. The Public Policy Institute won the 2010 AJLI Leadership Development Award and is being used as a model for Junior Leagues all over the country. It was a great accomplishment.

Now I am fully aware that this story is not an actual work story. But I readily tell others that I learned to lobby in the Junior League. Because I did. Recalling my personal story for a moment, I went to law school and practiced land-use law full time. While land-use law in Los Angeles is a relatively political practice, and I had been registered as a city lobbyist, the reality was that I did not do the lobbying. I was the behind the scenes; I was the technician. My experience with the Junior League was a turning point in my career; it taught me that I could make things happen on my own, that I could effectively predict the motivations of others, and that I could strategically use technical factors to benefit my clients.

I also learned that all the details matter, and you can't do everything the day of the event. You need lead time, and you have to plan. You have to lay everything down early to make sure all of the possibilities are addressed and establish how important things—like votes—can sometimes be as important as little things—like agenda placement. My opponents didn't realize this. They also failed to effectively plan for the weaknesses in their program. The president's leadership program was expensive, and she had done nothing to reduce the overall cost except to attempt to subsidize the cost at the last minute; her program relied heavily on outside professional leadership consultants that cost between five and ten thousand dollars annually. She spotted a problem, but it was too late. Instead of institutionally reducing the cost of the program, she just let it sail, figuring the program would be so popular that it would be funded.

I think there is another lesson here, as well. Nothing is black and white, ever. This is a story of two training programs within the context of a nonprofit organization; not a battle of good versus evil. There had to be a winner and a loser, in part because the president's program had no way to reduce its net cost. I wouldn't have had to take the actions I did if she had effectively done the leg work on her end that I did on my end to try and ensure program survival. And that was a lot of work. I spent a lot of time with September brainstorming how we were going to save the program. We would meet or talk on the phone and talk through our ideas for how we could get the same skills to the women in the program at a cheaper price, how we could reduce costs, and how we would structure the program and the related supporting materials. We would go and investigate thoughts and ideas and circle back to share what we learned and establish a best approach moving forward. We knew reduction in costs was a key component, but it wasn't the only component at issue. We had to rework the entire program over the course of a year. The president didn't want to do that with her program. She was proud of the program she had created, and effectively created an all-or-nothing scenario. The president's program was eventually revised and modified, but I think the lesson here is that you have to be willing to change to survive. When you go all-or-nothing, you risk everything.

One fact I regularly emphasize with newer members of our profession is that none of this is personal. I am often adversarial in many situations in the course of my career, and I made the mistake, early in my career, of treating my opponents like enemies, taking jabs personally, and using emotion to drive my work. While emotion is important, it is not an effective advocacy tool. Not only does it have the potential to blind you and lead you to ineffective decision-making, it also has the potential to burn bridges you may require in the future. Today's opponent is tomorrow's ally. Use your emotion in effective and efficient ways; creating enemies over trifles is not effective or efficient, and will actually make your job more difficult in the long haul.

I think the best career lesson from this story is that you never know what you are going to learn, and from where. Some of the most effective public policy advocates on behalf of maternal health and perinatal mood disorders in the United States worked with me in the Junior League—and they were not public policy advocates when they joined. They were insurance administrators, stay-at-home moms, and saleswomen. Coming to the League, they were exposed to a world that they loved and could also learn to make a difference, but they also learned to do something new and do it well. You never know what opportunities are out there unless you try, whether it is learning a new sport, joining a common interest group, or taking a class. My best source for details on our local school district is my mah jongg group. You never know what's out there. Hey, the Junior League is how I finally became a lobbyist!

Your journey will surely be different, but be open to where the Universe leads you, say yes to opportunities, and take care of yourself. I do hope you find the joy I have found in my life and through my career. It is not always easy, but it is almost always certainly worth the hard work. Feel free to reach out: I look forward to hearing from you.

> Nicole Kuklok-Waldman
> Instagram (@nkuklok)
> Twitter (@nicolekw)
> LinkedIn

9 CRISIS MANAGEMENT IN PUBLIC RELATIONS

Devon Nagle

 Devon Nagle is a senior vice president for HL Group in New York City. He is a strategic communications executive with extensive experience in external brand positioning, client service, marketing communications, employee engagement, crisis management, and media relations, with a specialty in writing and narrative development.

Nagle is particularly skilled at translating complex industry issues for a broad audience, leveraging a range of channels and communications disciplines. He has more than 20 years' worth of PR experience and has led successful communications campaigns for such brands as Expedia, Four Seasons, Google, Casper, Ralph Lauren, PepsiCo, the Michelin Guides, Stella Artois, MasterCard, and Sprint.

Part I: Personal

I became a publicist kind of by accident and kind of on purpose. I became a publicist by design because I wanted to be a writer. That panned out, if not in the way I imagined—since I started in PR in 1995, I've written a wealth of copy on a range of topics you missed entirely.

Writing is a part of the gig, and a big one—you shape words to explain your client's position to the world, or the world's position to your client. In that sense, I've become a writer, if you want to stretch the definition pretty unreasonably far. I've written more in an explanatory way than a creative way: countless memos and PowerPoint slides and talking points and speeches and statements and key messages and bios and questions and answers. I like writing, so if I get to do it in a way that is constricted by business constraints, it's still enjoyable. PR writing gets creative when you know what you're doing, especially when you're trying to make a case.

I became a publicist by accident when I graduated from Syracuse University in 1994 with a degree in English and textual studies. I took my first job at Shandwick Public Affairs, a Washington, DC, public affairs and PR firm, without a clear idea of what the job entailed. Public affairs is the effort to shape public policy, often by steering public opinion in a way that prompts the government to respond. Shaping public opinion, whether it's for policy purposes or to prompt the public to respond to a brand—buying its products or services over that of a competitor, for example—is very much central to the business.

This was 1995 when I began, so the tools of public relations were blunter and less effective than they are today. We faxed press releases to newspapers and magazines and called reporters to confirm they had received the announcement and to ask if they'd consider writing about it. We called a lot of people out of the blue and asked them for thirty seconds of their time. Sometimes they said yes, and you had thirty seconds to make your case. Often they said no. More often, they let the phone ring and ring.

The key, then and now, was to get to know the right writer and the influential editor. Even if the tools we use now have evolved, needing to know the right people hasn't changed. If the writers knew you, and recognized your number, they would answer. If they saw you as someone who was calling when the news was worth covering—someone who had given them information in the past that they'd found interesting and useful, someone they trusted—you'd have an easier time getting feedback: a yes, no, maybe, or maybe later.

In PR, you're being paid to solicit (hopefully positive) feedback from reporters, and among the more frustrating features of public relations is the fact that many reporters simply won't respond to your outreach. You can imagine why. If you are a reporter and your phone is ringing endlessly, your email is filling up, and you're being constantly solicited by hungry publicists, you'd tune them out, too. That being said, being a successful publicist requires that you build a network of reporters and editors and producers who trust you. If you can do this, then you leap ahead of thousands of publicists and have an easier time placing your story in the right place.

The tools have evolved from the days of the fax—a quaint machine that now sits mostly quiet in the corner of an office, unused. We email these days. We call reporters we know, occasionally those we don't. We pass messages to reporters we don't know through reporters we do. (Please know that I am using "reporter" as a placeholder—PR people try to connect with reporters, editors, publishers, producers, production assistants, bloggers, online influencers, you name it.) We leverage social media channels. We send direct messages via Twitter; sometimes we direct message through LinkedIn.

The more successful publicists learn to dial down the hyperbole when they communicate. The PR world is filled with hyperbole, as is the world in general. Many publicists think the trick to standing out is to shout louder, to pack messages with exclamatory claims. Revolutionary! Disruptive! Breakthrough! AMAZING!

This is a mistake, and an oft-repeated one. The right editor will understand at a glance if the story has merit. The more breathless you seem, the less likely you'll be taken seriously and the quicker your email address will end up in their spam folder.

From Then to Now

When I worked for the public affairs firm in 1995, I commuted to Washington, DC, from Baltimore. Eventually tiring of the commute, I left the firm and worked briefly for a DC-based not-for-profit, Share Our Strength. Share Our Strength is an anti-hunger organization, led by an inspiring leader in Billy Shore. Shore is a powerful DC influential who had left a career in politics to dedicate his life to the fight against hunger (look them up if you can, and donate; they do extraordinary work). A PR career dedicated to a social cause may not pay as well as one dedicated to corporate or consumer concerns, but you'll never wonder about the value of what you're doing. Pride of purpose is no small thing.

I wasn't at Share Our Strength for an extended stretch of time. Share Our Strength's head of PR was my former supervisor at Shandwick Public Affairs; she offered me a short-term role in their PR department while the existing publicist was on maternity leave, with the tacit understanding that I would be seeking a new position closer to home.

Eventually, I found a position at Shandwick in Baltimore, ten minutes from my apartment. I worked on a range of accounts, spanning telecom, business-to-business, and corporate. One client introduced the nation's first all-digital wireless telecom service.

We promoted this new service by arranging the nation's first digital telephone call between then-Vice President Al Gore and Baltimore Mayor Kurt Schmoke, which was meant to echo the very first phone call, made from Alexander Graham Bell to his assistant, Thomas Watson, in 1876. Mayor Schmoke noted that "in 1843, the very first telegraph was sent from Baltimore to Washington" and joked that he appreciated Washington "finally returning our message."

My time at Shandwick was filled with enjoyable firsts. I met senators. I joined the company's beer-league softball team. I traveled to Las Vegas for the first time. I loved it (the company, not Las Vegas. Las Vegas is awful).

After three years in Baltimore, I longed to return home. I was raised in Connecticut and had always imagined that I would make my career in New York City. I knew a man, Alex Stanton, who ran a PR firm in New York City—I'd met him in at my first job. He hired me. I moved in with college friends at an apartment in Brooklyn in 1999 and began work for Stanton Crenshaw Communications.

I've worked in New York City ever since. Eventually I left Stanton Crenshaw for a higher title at Waggener Edstrom. From there I moved to MWWPR, as the vice president of writing services. It was a fun job. I wrote full time, for a range of clients on a range of topics. I wrote op-eds, blog posts, press releases, and position papers. I wrote an e-book. I'd gotten the position at MWWPR because I'd worked with a high-level MWWPR executive at a previous agency. As with editors and producers, you will build a network of colleagues over the course of your career, people you like or admire (or dislike but respect), and that network will help you find your path forward.

The MWWPR position didn't last; when the agency experienced a downturn, they quite rightly decided they no longer needed a full-time writer on a vice president's salary, and I was laid off. This was a professional and personal shock. I was told one afternoon that the office's managing director needed to see me. When I entered his office, I saw that he was sitting alongside the head of human resources, and my heart stopped, then started, then sank.

Within fifteen minutes, I was out of the building. I didn't have time to say goodbye to friends in the office. I didn't even have my own cell phone; I had used one provided by the firm. I had to call my wife, Caroline, from a Manhattan pay phone to give her the news. A week later, we learned she was pregnant with our first child.

I spent six months looking for a job, exercising regularly (a small silver lining of unemployment is that you can work out at the gym when it's empty) and working on a book, which quite rightly remains unpublished. Eventually I secured an interview through a friend and former colleague with Hamilton South, the head of HL Group—a powerful and well-connected PR firm that was best known for specializing in fashion and luxury.

Hamilton wanted to start a consumer and lifestyle division at HL Group, and chose me to do so. My first hire was Dave McNamee, a bright and motivated former colleague at MWWPR. Dave and I made another hire, and another, and another. The division was built, in large part, on the back of Expedia, one of the world's largest travel sites. Expedia was the first client I managed at HL Group, and grew to become the largest account within the company.

The account grew slowly but steadily. At first we handled all communications within the United States. Then we became the global agency of record. Then we began managing the company's social media channels. Then we opened a technology division, then added a corporate division, and onward.

Over the past eight years, my division has represented a pretty expansive range of clients. Consumer and lifestyle is a wide category; you can fit almost anything within it if you want to. We've been the global agency of record for Four Seasons Hotels and Resorts. We've represented different brands within Anheuser Busch, including Stella Artois and Beck's. We've worked with billion-dollar start-ups Casper and Houzz, and the legendary fashion brand Ralph Lauren.

We've executed a series of campaigns for Google—including one during the 2014 football (soccer) World Cup. Google can measure a country's collective emotional state by analyzing its Google searches. That year, the World Cup host country, Brazil, was unexpectedly routed by eventual champion, Germany, 7–1. Google (and the reporters we put alongside them) watched Brazil go from a state of euphoria to a state of despair, in real time, over the course of 90 minutes.

We threw chef-studded parties in New York, San Francisco, and Chicago for the Michelin Guides. We promoted Jaguar/Land Rover cars and SodaStream's first-ever Super Bowl ad campaign.

For one year we represented world tennis #1-ranked player Novak Djokovic (I never met him, only his management.) We represented a small Alabama whiskey in Clyde May's and a global French liqueur in Grand Marnier. We hosted events at the Cannes Film Festival, Sundance, and the Toronto International Film Festival. We threw small tasteful dinners and lavish spectacles. We worked with celebrities, with billionaire business leaders, with politicians, and with online influencers whose Instagram feeds reach millions.

For me, Expedia helped make this possible. As their global and US agency of record, we worked on just about every facet of their communications. We executed multicountry studies examining how many vacation days are given to workers in different countries, how many they take, and why. (In a nutshell, Europeans are given, and take, the most vacation, while Asians take the fewest. American vacation habits more closely mirror the Japanese than the French.) We announced that the residents of Germany are the most likely to sunbathe nude at the beach; that Italians are the most fearful of sharks; and that the least popular airline passenger is the rear seat-kicker, narrowly edging the inattentive parent.

We helped reporters cover the impact of tsunamis, oil spills, and earthquakes on travelers in different countries. We launched new products, sent bloggers and influencers on trips, and identified the most interesting travel destinations and the best techniques to book travel to reach them.

Occasionally, and memorably, we took a position on social issues. This is not a new phenomenon; major brands have long been encouraged to weigh in on the issues of the day. Most decline to do so. The rise of social media has made engagement more of a priority, rather than less.

It's tricky, of course. No matter the issue, by taking a stand on it you will inevitably place yourself in opposition to many millions of people. Republicans and Democrats all buy flights and rent hotel rooms, after all. In 2012, Expedia chose to take a position. What follows is a case study in what happened when they did.

Part II: Crisis Management Case Study: Expedia, "Find Yours," and Dealing With an Angry Public

This case study is an exercise in crisis management.[1] Not all crisis PR fits into the same category. There are crises that happen in the moment: an accident, an executive accused of malfeasance, a misstep on social media that goes viral, a customer service snafu, you name it. There are crises that are slower builds: a company acquires another and elects to lay off a number of employees, a brand campaign incurs the

---

1. My use of the phrase "dealing with an angry public" is a reference to a book published by MIT professor Lawrence Susskind. Susskind taught a two-day course in Boston that I found particularly useful. In it, he teaches publicists how to engage with opponents who are angrily opposed to their point of view—how to find common ground, in essence.

fury of an outside group, a company finds itself under legal scrutiny, or a hacker infiltrates an organization and exposes data. The steps to manage each are also not uniform—sometimes you apologize, sometimes you don't. Social media, of course, allows pretty much any crisis to spiral wildly—someone takes offense, shares with friends, and suddenly, the offending brand is ubiquitous, facing boycotts and furious inquiries. This case study is an example of the latter. My client Expedia took public steps that we knew would provoke a backlash. This is how we managed it.

In 2012, Expedia introduced a new brand campaign, "Find Yours." The company worked with a Los Angeles-based advertising agency to create it. The purpose of "Find Yours" was to celebrate the *emotion* of travel, not merely the process of booking it. Expedia helps millions of people book travel every day—you use the site to research flights and hotels, rent cars, identify activities, you name it. With "Find Yours," Expedia wanted to remind people that the website didn't merely help you rent a hotel room—it helped people make memories that lasted a lifetime.

"Find Yours" featured a series of television and online advertisements—videos, mostly—that explored how travel transforms people. In the company's words:

> [Find Yours] features 100% user-generated content, or, more specifi-
> cally, travel-generated content—photos and videos and stories from every-
> day consumers, explaining how travel has transformed them. This content
> is featured throughout all facets of the campaign, which will include a new
> 60-second TV spot, as well as a series of mini-documentaries and short
> travel-themed films from up-and-coming filmmakers. Find Yours will also
> become Expedia's new tagline, replacing "Where You Book Matters."

These videos featured real people (versus actors) who had been changed in some way through travel. Finding them was a challenge; Expedia worked with a Los Angeles-based advertising agency to build the campaign, and the agency worked for months on end to find candidates. Eventually they succeeded.

Our goal for "Find Yours" was awareness. We wanted the campaign to be seen by as many people as possible, through as many channels as possible. We wanted people to click on the YouTube link and watch the video. We wanted people to read about it, to watch coverage of it on television, to share it with their friends. Fortunately for us, the campaign was built in such a way as to encourage sharing. It was heartwarming without being schmaltzy, inspiring without being overbearing.

One "Find Yours" video featured a father at an amusement park ride with his young son. Homemade video shows the son and dad gleefully spinning in circles. In voiceover, the father said, "In that moment, I realized *that's my boy*. This is my life. And I've only got one of each."

One video centered on a woman, Maggie, who had been helped by St. Jude Children's Research Hospital. She had cancer as a child, and the doctors at St. Jude helped save her life. A fellow patient she met at St. Jude, Odie, did not survive. The three-minute video details Maggie's memories of Odie and the strength that he helped her find.

"Find Your Understanding" is the subject of this case study. This three-minute video follows Artie Goldstein, the retired father of Jill. Artie admits to discomfort over Jill's homosexuality. When Jill's partner, Nikki, approached Artie to ask for his permission to marry Jill, Artie was apprehensive.

"My expectation of what Jill's life was going to be included a husband," Artie said. "So when Nikki came to ask permission to marry our little girl, that startled me. I told her, 'This is not the dream I had for my daughter.' I didn't say yes, I didn't say no."

Jill and Nikki work in advertising, and had, fortuitously, captured gorgeous video of their marriage ceremony. Artie traveled to their wedding and explained, in voiceover, that the experience changed him.

"When we got to California, and we saw how happy they were, all that trepidation just seemed to go away. That was a big turning point. Of course, walking Jill down the aisle, just looking at her, she was breathtaking, beautiful. Julie [my wife] and I were just swelling with emotion. You come to terms with it and you say, this is the natural order of things in your life, and it's supposed to be this way."

The video was lovely, beautifully shot and tastefully executed. Our challenge in PR was what to do with it. There's a category of media that covers brand campaigns: *Ad Age* and *Adweek* exist to celebrate—or excoriate—company ads.

This was different. The issue of gay marriage was roiling the American landscape in 2012. What Expedia had created was a statement of support in favor of gay marriage, which put them squarely into the fight.

I am a progressive. I share the company's point of view. But in your career, it may not always be this way. You might end up representing a company that takes positions on social issues that differ from yours. You might find yourself in diametric opposition to the CEO of a client. The decision of what to do in that case rests with you, and there's no easy answer. Public relations firms represent brands of all size and stripe. Big Tobacco, oil and gas, firearms manufacturers—these can often be high-paying clients, and the agency's financial well-being may be pegged to their success.

It is often easier to work in-house; in that instance, you can choose the kinds of companies that you represent, based on shared values. At an agency, you might not always have that luxury. My advice in that case is to approach your supervisor at the outset of a relationship and let him or her know that you cannot represent that client in good faith. It's easier to replace you on the account in the beginning than it is further down the road.

With "Find Your Understanding," our job was to find a reporter at an influential media outlet before the video went live, and to offer them the exclusive. An exclusive is just as it sounds: you give the story to one writer or producer and agree that they will be the first to cover it.

A second technique is called embargoed outreach. You reach out to a series of media contacts and let them know that you have a story that may interest them, and if they agree to honor the embargo (i.e., to agree not to publish the story before a given date) then you'll give them the relevant details. Some news outlets disdain the embargo; the *Wall Street Journal*, for one, doesn't accept them. The *New York Times* tends to be reluctant; they prefer exclusives. But many media outlets will agree to an embargo. You'll share the information with them privately and they'll tell you whether they like it or not. The purpose of embargoed outreach is to create a groundswell of coverage on the day your client makes the formal announcement, often via press release.

Groundswells make the story move. If a half dozen influential media outlets cover the same story within a short period of time, other outlets will follow suit (and some journalists will complain to you privately that you didn't contact them earlier). You want a story to begin to move on its own, for journalists to spot it in a competing publication and decide to cover it.

The purpose of an exclusive is the same. You pick exclusive targets based on their influence. The morning shows—Good Morning America and *TODAY* are the top two—will put your story in front of millions on day one. As such, they're often very picky about which stories they take and which they do not. The key in that instance is to know the right producers. As noted earlier, your personal and professional networks will greatly impact your success.

We chose the *Huffington Post* as our exclusive target for "Find Your Understanding." In the week leading up to the day Expedia published the video on its social channels—YouTube and Vimeo—I engaged with an editor at the *Huffington Post*'s "Gay Voices" vertical. He accepted the exclusive and was given an early look at the video, as well as the opportunity to interview the video's stars Artie, Jill, and Nikki.

He published the story at the same time Expedia published the video, and the world reacted immediately. The story started to move. When the exclusive ran, our team at HL Group was pitching widely, sharing the video, the announcement and the backstory with a wide range of press. Coverage was near-immediate, across a range of verticals. LGBT publications celebrated Expedia's decision to support gay marriage. The advertising trades applauded as well.

When Expedia eventually began running the video as a television commercial, the *New York Times* wrote a print article headlined, "Commercials With a Gay Emphasis Are Moving to Mainstream Media," featuring an image from "Find Your Understanding." It read, in part:

> When Expedia decided to begin running on television this month a commercial it had introduced online in October, about a father's trip to attend his daughter's wedding to another woman, the media plan was drawn up to include Logo, the cable channel aimed at gay and lesbian viewers. But the commercial is also running on networks watched by general audiences, like CNN, History, MSNBC and the National Geographic Channel.

"As we were making our Web site more personal, we wanted to get back to the idea that travel is really personal," said Sarah Gavin, director for public relations and social media at Expedia in Seattle, and "equality is a core part of who we are."

The Expedia decision is indicative of a significant change in how marketers are disseminating ads with so-called L.G.B.T. themes, for lesbian, gay, bisexual and transgender. For the last two or three decades, such ads were usually aimed at L.G.B.T. consumers, placed in media those consumers watch and read, and then supplemented with tactics that included event marketing like floats in Pride Month parades.

By all measures, we'd achieved our goals. We'd earned massive national and regional coverage spanning online, print, and broadcast. The video earned millions of views. The groundswell we'd engineered at the outset of the campaign had done its job, putting the video and its backstory in front of a wide set of journalists, many of whom covered it.

That wave of coverage, of course, reached millions of people who did not share Expedia's convictions. Shortly after the *Huffington Post* article appeared in October of 2012, we started receiving direct feedback from consumers themselves. Some were thrilled, and chose to email me and my team directly to say so.

Many were not. My team managed the "PR alias" for Expedia. Reporters interested in speaking with Expedia often went directly to the alias to email Expedia for comment. (Many emailed my team directly, once they came to know us, but others emailed the PR alias.)

That PR alias was then obviously accessible to anyone who visits Expedia.com. Soon, we began receiving inbound emails from people who had seen the video and wanted to express their anger.

It is important to note that support or opposition of gay marriage is not simply a good/bad proposition. While I support gay marriage, the Catholic church does not. A high number of religious Americans reached out to us to communicate this. The emails ranged in tone. Some were feverish denunciations of gay marriage as an institution, and of Expedia in supporting it. Some expressed concern that these videos and commercials were viewed by children: How, they asked, were they supposed to address this with their kids? Some commenters were confused: Why was a company that sells flights and hotels suddenly behaving like an activist? Many of those messages concluded with a note saying that Expedia had lost their business for good.

As a rule, we did not respond, and rarely received more than one email from the same person. If we began exchanging points of view with angry strangers—and gave them our personal email and phone number in doing so—we'd open up a line of communication that we'd be powerless to close. This exposed one of the ironies of public relations: you very rarely actually engage with the public. Mostly, you work with the press, and reach the public through them.

Expedia's Facebook page was flooded on day one with positive posts, with a few complaints sprinkled in. Eventually, the tide turned, and more and more commenters arrived on the page to threaten a boycott. We realized quickly that this was an organized effort—a great many comments used the exact same terminology in the same order. An institution on the Christian Right—whether it was a church, a media organ, or some other institution (we never learned)—was organizing the pushback, encouraging its adherents to go to this page and post these words.

Soon, the leader of a faith-based "family" organization in Florida elected to reach out to HL Group directly. He started faxing angry notes to the office, to the attention of our founders. He claimed he was going to hire a plane and fly it over Expedia headquarters in Seattle, with a banner attached asking Expedia why they supported the breakdown of the family.

We informed Expedia immediately. I didn't take the threat particularly seriously; the fact that he used a fax somehow made the threat comical. But you never know. Someone who takes the time to do this might also take the time to fly to Seattle and walk into Expedia headquarters. They alerted security.

Nothing came of it. One reason the larger situation did not escalate further was our collective decision to stay the course. Often, companies will react to the threat of a boycott by quickly reversing course, hoping to placate the angry mob. Sometimes it works. Often, it simply angers everyone—supporters feel betrayed, opponents feel victorious, and everyone walks away feeling badly about the brand in question.

This is one key takeway in crisis communications: the world will keep spinning. Outrage will flare and then subside. People move on. It's what you do in the moment that dictates how long the flame will burn, and how brightly. Corporate indignance—a refusal to admit an obvious mistake—will cause a crisis to deepen.

If a company makes a mistake of some sort, then of course an apology and a course correction is appropriate. Expedia did not view its position as a mistake. They knew gay marriage was a contentious issue and chose to add their voice to the debate. This was a measured decision, made over months and months and supported at the highest levels of the company. They believed that they were on the right side of history.

We also knew that outrage is fleeting. The groups that organized the collective response quickly moved on to new targets. The Florida faith faxer was probably pumping out dozens of such faxes every day, hoping for a response. When we didn't give him one, he moved on, and life returned to normal.

Expedia had the courage of its convictions. It's an important point, because public opinion will shift back and forth, and if you react to each shift, you'll end up whipsawed. People do not respect a brand that seems determined to please all people all of the time. People respect conviction.

Devon Nagle
Senior Vice President
HL Group Consumer & Lifestyle Division
Instagram: @devonjnagle

10 EVENT PLANNING AND PUBLIC RELATIONS

Gineen Cargo

Originally from Charlotte, North Carolina, Gineen Cargo is a PR strategist and meeting and event planning professional with over 10 years of experience executing strategic communications initiatives in corporate, academic, and PR agency arenas. She is a certified meeting professional, certified wedding planner, and the owner of Cargo & Co. Events, a wedding and special event planning company. Gineen holds a bachelor's degree in mass communication from North Carolina Central University and a master's degree in strategic communication from American University. Currently, she is the Wells Fargo Endowed Chair with the department of mass communication at North Carolina Central University.

Part I: Personal

People often ask me, "How did you get into PR?" The honest answer? I believe I was born a publicist. Throughout my life I've always promoted things. If it wasn't the newest show on television, it was the latest toy. I have been told that I had the gift of gab at an early age. As a publicist, one of the most important things is to learn how to be observant. I'm told that I was born with my eyes wide open, ever observant, looking around and taking things in. As being observant is a key characteristic trait of a PR pro, I guess one could say the PR life chose me! Growing up I was obsessed with pop culture and often spent my time watching *60 Minutes*, *Ricki Lake*, and *Oprah*. I always found myself reading magazines in the grocery store while my mom shopped and prided myself on knowing what was going on in the news, pop culture entertainment, and politics with a genuine interest and love of how it all intersected.

I decided in my senior year in high school that I would major in English in college. After a whirlwind tour of colleges up and down the East Coast of the United States, and from my childhood obsession with TV shows like *The Cosby Show*, *A Different World*, and *Living Single*, I realized wanted to attend a historically black college and university (HBCU), following in the footsteps of my parents. Much to my mother's dismay, as a graduate of the HBCU North Carolina A&T

University in Greensboro, North Carolina, I decided to attend a rival school, my father's alma mater, North Carolina Central University (NCCU).

In August of 2000 I packed my bags and headed to the illustrious camps of NCCU determined to be an English major, with the goal of being an editor for a publication like *Essence, People,* or *Seventeen Magazine.* However, I found out quickly that even though I was a bookworm, the idea of studying Shakespeare and other literary greats just didn't excite me. So I began to explore a related area of focus: media studies. With this concentration, I began to take classes like Mass Media and Society, Writing for TV and Radio, and Intro to Mass Communication to attempt to figure out how to mesh my love for news, radio, entertainment, and mass media. After dabbling in photography with the school's student-run paper the *Campus Echo* and having a radio show on AudioNet, the student-run campus radio station, I decided to return to Charlotte for the summer after my freshman year to intern in radio promotions. Later in my undergrad years I spent time interning with K97.5 FM, a radio station in Raleigh. After completing my core courses and exploring broadcast journalism, the NCCU Mass Communication department embarked on an expansion. In my senior year, the department added a new concentration: mass communication.

During the spring semester before senior year I found out that many of my friends and peers at NCCU were planning a summer in New York City to complete internships and have a fun summer exploring the Big Apple. I decided I wanted to spend the summer in NYC too! My parents agreed, under the condition that I could find a way to pay for living in the ever-expensive city. I spent hours on AOL and Yahoo searching for an internship, and lo and behold I found an internship in PR . . . whatever that was . . . at the Studio Museum in Harlem paying $260 every two weeks. I'd hit the jackpot! I spent the summer touring famous museums like the Met, planning a special summer series of events for the Studio Museum; having my photographs of the Harlem community published in various magazines; hobnobbing with museum elites like Thelma Golden, and amazing then-artists-in-residence like Kara Walker and Kehinde Wiley (Google them); and promoting the museum, its galleries, and amazing curated collections. I returned to NCCU in the fall with new skills and a renewed energy to graduate and embark on the path toward a career in PR. That spring I landed a PR internship with a local agency, French West Vaughn, and was tasked with managing campaigns for Wrangler Jeans and one of my favorite clients to date: the Central Intercollegiate Athletic Association (CIAA). It was exciting creating and executing a pageant contest that would be conducted during the CIAA tournament for a longstanding brand and association. This combination of exciting internship experiences reinforced my interest in being in the mix of the craziness of the communications world. I learned that I loved being a behind-the-scenes PR oro, without the high-profile visibility required of a journalist or radio disc jockey.

Historically, large metropolitan areas like New York, Los Angeles, and Chicago hold the largest share of jobs in public relations, and yet I've learned that every city or small town in the US has a need for public relations professionals too. Whether you find yourself working in development and fundraising, internal communications for a corporate company, or at an agency, it's not hard to find an open position within the field of public relations. The need for PR also extends globally as many countries, like China and the United Kingdom, are in tune with the need for public relations and global communications. I've worked in major NYC and Washington, DC, markets and I'm currently in a smaller market working at an agency in Raleigh, North Carolina.

When I graduated from NCCU in May of 2004, I had trouble finding a job in communications and began working in financial services for the Vanguard Group in Charlotte. I noticed a void of communication-focused jobs available at an entry level in North Carolina, and decided to try living in a larger city. After a year in finance, I landed a job at Discovery Communications, based in Silver Spring, Maryland, a suburb of the Washington, DC area. At Discovery, I was responsible for media planning and buying for major networks like TLC and Animal Planet. It was there that I honed my skills in advertising and media planning, and learned how those areas of focus can influence and assist publicity and public relations efforts. After a corporate layoff at Discovery in 2006 I landed a job at American University, where I strategically sought out employment so that I could gain my master's degree. After an 18-month intensive weekend program with classes every Saturday from 9 a.m. to 5 p.m., I graduated with my master of arts in strategic communication. A few weeks before graduation, I landed a job at Stanley Black & Decker as the marketing communications manager for the company's major power tool brands: Black & Decker, Stanley, and Porter-Cable.

After a number of wonderful years at Stanley Black & Decker, I went back on the job market and am currently an account supervisor at G&S Communications. While there's no cool backstory to my current job (I simply applied and had a standard interview), one thing that stood out during the process was that even as a seasoned communicator with major brands under my experience belt and a master's degree, I still had to do a two-hour writing test to show my proficiencies in AP style, press release writing, and general communications correspondence in order to be considered for employment.

In addition to being an account supervisor at a PR agency, I am the Wells Fargo Endowed Chair and an adjunct professor at North Carolina Central University. This appointed position is rewarding as it gives me the opportunity to flex a new muscle as an industry practitioner and faculty member. I'm able to interact with students who are beginning to explore the possibilities of being a PR pro. As NCCU is a HBCU, I'm able to inspire and challenge students of color to embark into the communications field by full of information and experience in the field through robust internship opportunities. As an industry practitioner I bring in industry executives, guest speakers, media influencers, and human relations reps to speak to the students about best practices for getting and maintaining a job in the field. I also challenge students to do as much research as possible to learn if PR is truly for them. I love being an advocate for the inclusion of minorities in communications and a champion of my students' success. I'm here to highlight the challenges that exist while helping to showcase the world of PR.

With entering into a career in public relations, I found that I had to rethink my dreams of being the talent. However, I have been pleasantly surprised to find it *more* rewarding to be behind the scenes. For example, I'd be remiss if I didn't say I've sat one-on-one in rooms with cool public figures like Kanye West, Spike Lee, and Barbara Walters, as well as CEOs of major companies and corporations. Communication students with aspirations in the media limelight may find themselves conflicted with the thought of giving up dreams of being a Grammy award winning rapper, famous late-night show host and producer, actor, celebrated visual artist, celebrity entrepreneur, CEO, morning talk show host, high-profile journalist, or social media superstar. My counter is that on a daily basis you might find me, and many other PR pros, sitting with someone that holds one of those titles. More than likely, we PR pros are the ones entrusted to lead the charge on their publicity campaigns, crisis communications efforts, branding projects, and other various initiatives. As an added bonus, they know little old me, their public relations representative, by first name. And isn't that way cooler?

Yet the perks of a fun, sometimes high-profile job don't come without low points. After all, PR is often at the top of the list of the most challenging and stressful jobs in the world. In my career, the biggest forward-facing challenge I've experienced thus far has been the overall lack of diversity and inclusion in the workplace within the world of communications. As an African American female under 40, I'm a unicorn. I have had to become comfortable and familiar with being the only female, millennial, and minority in the room. Ironically, I'm also usually one of the only ones with an advanced degree and with a breadth of well-rounded experience. With my foray into the PR field, I've discovered some additional interesting insights about it. Here are seven key insights I believe to be important considerations when thinking about diving into a career in the world of public relations.

Be a Champion of Diversity

Diversity in any industry is key. However, while diversity is the equivalent of being asked to the party, inclusion is being called out and asked to the floor to dance. While the field has made some strides in terms of being diverse, inclusion is lagging. Traditionally, PR was male-centered. I've found that over time the field has seemed to transition to be female, especially at the entry level. However, in terms of color, it seems to be a bit bland. Google a few local agencies and you *might* find a face or two of color. How do we combat it? There are seminars and conferences focused on what to do to bring about true change. Some of my colleagues have left the world of agency to hang out their hat as a solo practitioner. Let's challenge the industry to be truly diverse with inclusion of all colors, creeds, religions, beliefs, and backgrounds.

Relationships and Community Building Are Key

Relationships are everything in life, business, and especially PR. It is important that as you build media contact lists of editors, reporters, journalists, and bloggers you'd like to reach that you remind yourself to not just build contacts, but to build relationships. I have a group of past classmates, former coworkers, bosses, and people I've met in the industry who I refer to as my personal board of directors. These folks—some in PR/communications, some in other non–communication fields, and some who are influencers—often provide career insights and guidance. These people can see around corners I can't and often know people in places I need to reach who are happy to make connections. You too should curate a personal board of directors. By focusing on building a core of personal influencers, you will help form your personal brand and in turn will find help with pitching a client's or business's story. By surrounding yourself with others who force you to level up you'll improve yourself, which in

PR is a Process

PR is best described as a strategic process that requires patience, planning, and purpose. It simply doesn't happen overnight. Even viral campaigns take time to build. There is a value in staking small steps, using small stepping stones to cross a long and broad river. You will find that your bosses, clients, and C-suite executives often expect microwaved quick results with champagne tastes and minimal beer-flavored budgets.[1] In these times, be confident in explaining that PR *always* comes down to consistent strategy. The best PR pro will create goals, a realistic roadmap, and timeline and work as a counselor and company/client partner to assist, motivate, and provide strategies toward the end goal.

PR is Constantly Evolving

PR has evolved from just media relations to an integrated communications approach. Traditional PR consisted of compiling a list of media outlets and target editors, deploying a pitch, securing media hits, and counting and recording these hits. Now, PR is more integrated and the lines of PR, advertising and marketing are becoming more blurred. Traditional PR no longer exists. However, the core skills and competencies

---

1. C-suite gets its name from the titles of top senior executives, which tend to start with the letter C, for "chief," as in chief executive officer (CEO), chief financial officer (CFO), chief operating officer (COO), and chief information officer (CIO). Also called "C-level executives."

needed in PR are still relevant. These include writing, communication, attention to detail, media relations, being proactive, and having a strong work ethic.

Showcase Creativity to Kill Media Clutter

Creating creative content is a necessity. Curating content that will get the attention of your target audience is what leads to brand champions. Whether writing a blog, a social media post on Facebook or Instagram, or creating an internal newsletter, you must aim to make sure to break through the clutter to gain maximum attention and exposure. Each piece of content should aim to clear, concise and purposeful. Taking time to plan a proper content strategy is important. This includes the most popular piece of PR collateral: the press release. Unless you're representing Apple or some other groundbreaking product, it is a waste of time and resources to rely solely on a press release for coverage. Press releases and pitches can no longer be used as stand-alone outreach. Depending on the topic you're pitching or key targeted outlets, some journalists will prefer a formal release, but only as a formality.

Always Have an Elevator Speech

The one-minute verbal pitch is now popular in our culture as we are all hard pressed for time. There's a reason why there are a crop of reality shows that focus on the quick pitch; fast-paced shows like *The Voice* and *Shark Tank* are more popular than ever. Whether it's selling a product or selling yourself, it's helpful to have a planned and canned speech about what you're pitching always ready and accessible in your back pocket. There's power in being able to quickly and succinctly speak about the value you, your PR client, or your product offers.

Self-Care is a Need, Not Want

In PR, stress is brought on by client demands, tight deadlines, C-suite demands and expectations, the 24-hour news cycle, and social media melees and public scrutiny, as well as long and unsociable hours. According to several annual reports, PR consistently ranks in the top five or ten most stressful careers. The methodology used to rank PR's standing includes considering stress factors including travel, deadlines, public scrutiny, physical demands, environmental conditions, risk to life, and interactions with the public. To combat this, I've been forced to learn to value the art of self-care. Whether it's long walks, planning a vacation, or indulging in massages or breathing exercises, it is imperative to find coping mechanisms to deal with the pressures on any workplace.

In short, what I now know is that passion and dedication will take you places your degree cannot. Persistence and resilience in pitching, career searching, and networking is necessary. Like baseball, sometimes it takes the third pitch to hit a home run. Explore your likes through internships. As you progress in your career, be familiar and comfortable with being insecure. It's okay to not know where you're going postgraduation, or what you're doing. It's fine if you don't understand a concept or how to apply a theory you learned in your undergrad years on your first job. Be okay with saying "I don't know"—but then find out! Above all else, simply do your best. And remember: PR is not all glitz, glam, and fame, but boy is it fun.

Part II: Professional Event Planning Case Study for Black & Decker

When launching a product or service to the consumer or business market, an event is a useful way to create buzz and excitement. In the world of PR, a product launch event is a perfect opportunity to put the item you're promoting into the hands of an editor, journalist, reporter, or blogger. By inviting the media, the sheer publicity of a product launch event may generate coverage, which will ensure that the publics or stakeholders you're attempting to reach will become familiar with your product, potentially leading to awareness and engagement.

The Challenge

In 2012, Black & Decker®, a consumer power tool company, developed and brought to market GYRO™, the world's first motion-activated screwdriver. The screwdriver, which incorporated gyroscopic technology for controlling variable speed and direction, was an innovative product that merged the worlds of home improvement, mobility, and gaming together as one. The consumer power tool, home improvement, and gaming industries needed to be made aware of this new product and the innovative direction an old company was taking.

Black & Decker stood to compete with multiple industries and consumer products launching products to market daily. Many of these products focused on utilizing newfound technologies and innovative solutions for consumer paint points specific to the home improvement and power tool industry. Yet there was a void of innovative products that could be used effectively.

The Black & Decker marketing communications (MarCom) team aimed to utilize special event planning, a niche area within public relations that is an effective public relations tool, for its product launch campaign, supporting activations, and promotions to merge the gap between consumer, the power tool industry, and the media.

The Product

The GYRO was a screwdriver that used gyroscopic technology (think the Nintendo Wii) to respond to a user's movement. Ever heard the screwdriver adage "righty tighty–lefty loosey" to tell you which way to screw in something? With the GYRO, a user only needed to move his or her wrist slightly left or right to drive a screw in or out. With traditional rechargeable screwdrivers users are typically required to engage a switch for a direction change and are not offered variable speed. This screwdriver was an industry category first to market, as the screwdriver featured gyroscopic technology. As Black & Decker® sought to bring innovation to the screw driver category of home improvement, an innovative campaign was needed in order to launch this industry first product.

The Audience

We designated our targeting to be focused on innovative audiences and publics. After all, Black & Decker has built-in brand loyalists with an affinity for the brand, but there was a challenge to see what new, early adopter, or consumer audiences could be reached.

For the purposes of the GYRO product launch campaign, our target audience included men and women between the ages of 18 and 60 who were home improvement enthusiasts, crafters, DIYers, gamers, those interested in technology, and retirees with or without mobility issues.

Media

While we targeted many major news outlets and their technology or home improvement sections, other main media outlets we sought to reach included gaming and technology (*TechCrunch*, *WIRED*); science and technology (*Popular Science, Popular Mechanics*); male-focused publications (*Men's Fitness*); general interest (*Buzzfeed*); and home improvement (*The Family Handyman, This Old House Magazine, DIY, Better Homes and Gardens*).

Consumer

In addition to the usual consumer power tool target—men—we also focused on reaching home improvement enthusiasts and the female DIY decorator. These were newly discovered audiences to target along with the elderly, persons with disabilities surrounding mobility, diabetics, and gamers. With an aim to reach such diverse audiences, it was a natural fit to participate in a large-scale consumer product event to reach consumers.

The Approach

Historically, Black & Decker was known and celebrated for powerful products used to get work done, efficiently and reliably. We centered on leveraging the message of innovation and using that to launch the product over a series of small events. These product launch began in April 2012 with smaller events and led up to January 2013, where we attended the biggest electronic and technology focused trade show in the United States, the Consumer Electronics Show (CES).

The Black & Decker MarCom team that was focused on PR efforts was small. It consisted of myself, a senior vice president, and an intern. Together we planned a series of events, including and media one-on-one meetings (also known as desksides). Additionally, I executed a distribution of media kits, mailed to a list of nighttime TV personalities including Jimmy Kimmel, Conan O'Brian, Jimmy Fallon, and Jay Leno.[2] Additionally, the Black & Decker MarCom team made plans to attend the National Homebuilder's Trade Show and the Consumer Electronics Trade Show, both in Las Vegas, to give potential consumers and media professionals the opportunity to put their hands on the actual product.

Results

At the conclusion of the campaign the Black & Decker PR team coordinated and executed over six media-focused events where editors were able to see product demonstrations and were able to take home the product to test out for themselves. Over the course of the GYRO product launch campaign, there were over 100 million impressions in earned media. The biggest media hits included mentions on the *Rachel Ray Show*, the *Wendy Williams Show*, *The View*, *This Old House TV*, *Better Homes and Gardens*, *Men's Journal*, *Popular Science*, and *Popular Mechanics*. Additionally, the most well received media mention was the product won the 2012 Product of the Year by Time Magazine which has the world's largest circulation for a weekly news magazine with an estimated readership of 26 million. This campaign was a major success and the product continues to be marketed, promoted, and available for purchase at home improvement stores nationwide.

Gineen Cargo
Wells Fargo Endowed Chair
Owner, Cargo & Co. Events
gineen.cargo@nccu.edu
hello@cargoandcoevents.com
919-446-3360

---

2. A media kit is a promotional public relations tool that can serve several functions, including promoting the launch of a new company, or promoting the launch of a new product or service by an existing company. Fun fact: I received a series of personal phone calls from Jay Leno himself. During the calls, Leno expressed thanks for being sent a product kit that included GYRO™ and was excited about the product's innovation and ease of use!

11

BRANDING IN PUBLIC RELATIONS

Jacqueline Camacho-Ruiz

Jacqueline Camacho-Ruiz is a PR practitioner focusing on branding, company growth, and strategic development. She is currently the director of JJR, one of the fastest growing marketing and public relations agencies in Chicago's west suburbs. In addition, Jackie is founder of the Fig Factor Foundation, focused on unleashing the amazing in young Latinas, and the creator of the Today's Inspired Latina book series and international movement.

She is actively involved in the community through her current and past service on the boards of Publicity Club of Chicago, Junior Achievement– Western Region, Community Contacts, YWCA, Aurora Hispanic Heritage Board, Fox Valley Entrepreneurship Center, and the Fig Factor Foundation, among others. As a two-time cancer survivor, Jacqueline possesses wisdom about life well beyond her years. Finally, she is one of the few Latina small airplane pilots in the United States.

Part I: Personal

The Journey Begins in School

I was only 14 years old when my family immigrated to the United States from Mexico. The United States was quite a culture shock, but I was determined to master English as quickly as I could. By the end of my first year I was completely fluent, and also began studying German as my third language while in high school. After graduation, I enrolled in the nearby College of DuPage (COD) and pursued my associate's degree in business.

While in school I was working three jobs to support my family, since my dad had abandoned us when I was eighteen. It was difficult, but I continually dreamed of being an entrepreneur in the land of opportunities.

Then, at the age of 23 and just two weeks before my finals at COD, I was diagnosed with cancer, and then an additional pre-cancer, which led to the complete reconstruction of my digestive system. While devastating, I couldn't let this stop me. I was not only determined to survive, but graduate with honors and continue to build my business, JJR Marketing, Inc.

I asked the doctor, "Would you please let me get out of the hospital by next Thursday?" He smiled, knowing my dedication to my life's work, and replied "Yes—your positive attitude saved you, Jackie." I went to my finals with a tube draining my new digestive system, covered well under my clothes. Nobody ever found out, and I graduated with honors that semester.

The Pathway Is Not Always Straight

In 2006 I graduated from COD with my associate's degree in business, and I was already employed by Marriott and began climbing the ranks there. I was soon working as a sales executive at two Marriott properties making $26,000 annually. My path took a turn toward public relations when my sales position quickly morphed into a marketing position within a few months. My key responsibilities included outreach to local businesses to use our facility for accommodations and meetings. I had to create the contracts and send new clients their event and reservation details, as well as communicate all details to the rest of the staff.

I was happy with the work, but the environment I had first joined had changed. I have always been a very positive, upbeat energetic person and the combination of that, as well as being young, bred resentment among my coworkers. I wanted to work in an environment that supported my positivity, not drain me of it. This taught me a very important lesson: never stay in a job that you return home from every night in tears.

The night I quit my job at Marriott, my then boyfriend, who was a talented graphic artist able to put pictures to my words, took me out to dinner at a new Brazilian steakhouse called Chama Gaucha. We both loved the restaurant, and loved it even more after he proposed and I said yes. The next day, I went back to Chama Gaucha and offered to do their marketing. They were baffled, since they did not have anyone currently in charge of marketing (nor did they understand the importance of it). However, I loved the restaurant and was determined to show them my value. I asked them to give me any opportunity and eventually took the job of hostess.

I integrated myself into their culture and quickly picked up words, phrases, and even the "happy birthday" song in Portuguese. I would do my "market research," asking patrons about their experience, and I would return to my host stand to continue working on my marketing plan for the restaurant. Two weeks after starting, Chama Gaucha offered me a position in marketing with a small raise in salary. I was now making $32,000, which turned into $46,000 just six months later after I proved myself as the marketing manager. Eventually, I was in charge of three locations, making commission from groups that my assistants would book at each location. For three years, I was in charge of managing the $500K marketing budget for this $10 million dollar privately held company. I loved this job, since it allowed me to come up with ideas, create marketing campaigns, connect with the local community, invite leaders into the restaurant, and host events—it was everything I wanted.

A few years later I became pregnant with my son, and I knew that I would not be able to keep up the rhythm when he was born. I left the restaurant for personal reasons, but I had made amazing professional connections during my three years that would stay with me throughout my career. For example, I met many media outlets from both sales and the editorial side. I realized the importance of making connections with other leaders of influence in the community, and am nurturing those relationships still today. Now those people I met when marketing the restaurant are my media contacts to help my clients get press coverage. You never know who in your past will become your next mentor, boss, or partner in a business. One of my former high school English teachers is now a project manager in my book publishing company. I also have several former mentors who encouraged me initially with the growth of my business who are now well-paying clients. Never underestimate the power of your network.

Building My First Business

I started my marketing agency, JJR Marketing, Inc., in 2006 with a laptop that my husband gave me when we were dating. It was my first laptop, since I could not afford one on my own. From day one, I would rise every morning and get dressed as if I were going to a job, keeping the same consistency and professionalism as though I still had a boss. I have been working consistently in my business ever since that wonderful day when JJR Marketing was born.

There were a lot of naysayers when I started my business, including family. I heard things like, "You are too young," "You have no experience," and "How can you start a communications business when you did not even speak English a few years ago?" I didn't listen. I knew my network of restaurants and businesses from my work at Marriott and Chama Gaucha was the place to start. Before long, I had my first three clients, including other restaurants. When I opened shop in 2006, my goal was to have six clients by the end of 2007. I had 10 clients by the end of March 2007, due mostly, I believe, to my enthusiasm and love for what I was achieving for each one.

When I started out I was still young and figuring out who I was as a person, let alone a professional. This proved to be one of the biggest challenges: constantly adapting to new situations as a young Latina while deciphering who I was. I had a hard time being confident, embracing my cultural differences, and trusting in my abilities. I remember looking at myself in the mirror one day after being exhausted from pretending to be someone else and saying, "I love you Jackie . . . I love you the way you are." That was a turning point for me. I started truly living and embracing my Latina within.

After that, things started to flow. My authentic energy started to come out. I created synergy between the passion of my culture and genuine enthusiasm for helping others, and the pragmatic/systematic results approach my clients were looking for.

Despite my modest success I was still very young, and working in English, even though it was my second language. While I portrayed myself as someone confident in business, inside I was filled with self-doubt. As a marketing consultant, I was mainly working with much older Caucasian men in executive-level roles at various companies who sometimes didn't like or respect me, or just tried to intimidate me.

While there was always doubt, whenever I pitched an idea or presented creative work, my natural love for what I did shone through in the end. One time, a client remarked that I needed to hide my enthusiasm, or to tone it down. I was confused and hurt. How could I be other than I actually was? Shortly thereafter one of my mentors, who is a very successful executive coach, advised me not to listen. My enthusiasm was part of my uniqueness and what made me who I am. If the client didn't like it, so be it. This experience taught me that being authentic is always the way to go for both you and the client. I show that same enthusiasm in client meetings today.

My husband was my first coworker and partner, joining me in the business and enhancing all my creative work with his valuable skill. I was soon joined by a part-time content writer, an intern who proved herself amazing and is now a minority partner in the business, as well as a virtual team of about a dozen other strategic partners and creatives who help me fulfill visions for the client. I keep our virtual team close with regular conference calls, in-person quarterly meetings, and regular communication between us all. Together we win awards, do fabulous work, and make our clients as happy.

Since 2007 I have helped hundreds of companies in various industries, from start-ups to Fortune 500 companies, become vibrant entities that engage their audience and produce results. Usually, the start-up companies hire us to give them direction in their branding, go-to market strategies, new websites, and press releases to announce a new company to the media or to secure additional investors with the credibility of third-party endorsements. Bigger companies hire us for promotions and to position them as thought leaders in their industry, to reach out to the Hispanic market, or to create media placements opportunities. Our mission is to secure earned media placements by structuring their unique stories and matching them up to the interests of reporters and producers. We also are constantly listening to national trends in order to position our clients as experts on specific subjects. Local media outlets are always looking for someone to share an experience related to a national story.

We create ideas for our clients in a variety of ways. First, we bring the client to a discovery meeting to discuss the main objectives, budget, timeframe, and other items necessary to execute the campaign they want. People share their thoughts openly around the room and usually the winning idea is a combination of several ideas from different people. Then, it is up to us to make it happen. Other times, the ideas come up based on previous success or research, including competitive analysis, good old Google, or interviews with customers or team members. We take everything into consideration. If the client likes a certain direction of an idea, we keep exploring it until it is refined and ready for execution.

I have pursued my dream. I love it more every day, but most of all I love providing ideas to our clients that create results.

Part II: Professional Branding Case Study

The Challenge

Jim Oberhofer (Jim O.), National Hot Rod Association (NHRA) top fuel crew chief for Kalitta Motor Sports and author of *Top Fuel for Life: Lessons from a Crew Chief*, was referred to JJR Marketing for a very special project. In the broadest sense, Jim O. wanted to rebrand himself for a special cause.

Jim O. had gone through a dramatic life change following the death of his wife, Tammy. The once hard-drinking, fast-food-pounding, fast-living absent father who always put work first and family second was gone. Inspired by his wife's death and realizing he had a chance to change his ways, Jim O. set his life on a new course, reunited with his estranged daughter, took up ballroom dancing, lost weight, and started living a happier, healthier lifestyle. He even started a nonprofit organization in his wife's name, called the Tammy O. Foundation. By writing a book, he hoped to share his journey and lessons for life while raising money for the foundation, which benefits organizations that were near and dear to Tammy's heart such as BRAKES, Pandas International, Racers for Christ, DRAW, and Infinite Hero Foundation.

JJR was asked to help raise money for the book publishing process via a Kickstarter campaign. If successful, the campaign would fund the ghostwriting of the book and promote Jim O. as an author and speaker, all to benefit the Tammy O. Foundation. Most agencies would have said no, but we decided to take a chance. We committed to launching a 30-day Kickstarter campaign with the goal of raising $47,000.

Successfully executing a Kickstarter campaign is a risk that requires strategic planning, use of the right resources, innovative thinking, network activation, perseverance, and commitment. If the campaign did not meet the goal in 30 days, we would not be able to collect the partial pledges. It was an all-or-nothing type of campaign.

We established an aggressive schedule to launch the Kickstarter campaign in the next 30 days. This included the setup, administration, and all preliminary marketing components for the page itself.

The Solution

This campaign took everything JJR had in terms of manpower and marketing expertise. We first had to establish all the foundational marketing materials for the Kickstarter campaign page. That meant a working title of the book, a cover design to display on the page, advertising copy to persuade visitors to donate, and a teaser video that included an interview with Jim O. about his mission. JJR also assembled a team of "ambassadors" who agreed to help us promote the campaign the minute it was launched, and we worked with Kalitta to come up with fabulous incentives for the highest donors. These incentives included things like a VIP trip in the Kalitta jet to see an NHRA race, discarded auto parts straight from the pit, and a signed auto from NHRA racers. JJR was responsible for spelling out all of the details, rewards, and timeline of the campaign to ensure that we delivered what we promised. Throughout the 30-day campaign JJR had constant communication with the backers, so they would continue to trust us in the process.

From 30 days prior to the launch of the campaign, throughout the 30 days during the campaign run, I had nine out of my 14 team members working on promoting the link to the Kickstarter page and all the ongoing social media, ambassador communication, and media relations that needed to happen. I paid my team for two months before we knew we would actually raise the money. Because it was a Kickstarter campaign, if we came up $1,000 short of our $47,000 goal on the thirtieth day, we would receive nothing from the backers. It was the biggest risk I had ever taken in business, but I also learned to trust my gut feeling.

My motivation, more than anything, was that I believed in the project and truly wanted it to succeed. The clients trusted me because they knew we had their best interests in mind. Raising $47,000 seemed daunting and almost impossible, but something inside me told me to go for it. Jim's book was a gift the world needed to receive.

During this process I also learned to trust my team: to give them autonomy to be creative and present ideas. This was a huge project, and micromanagement was not an option. As a leader, you must learn to delegate and trust others. Every single one of them was crucial to the success of the campaign.

To make this happen, we also put into action my "five or more" rule to achieve success in marketing this campaign. The rule states that for every message you should be able to integrate at least five marketing/PR vehicles. For this project, following the rule meant continual touchpoints on the Kickstarter page, Twitter, press releases, Kalitta internal media, personal emails to ambassadors, and more. Businesses often don't think to disseminate their content as thoroughly as this, but during this campaign we needed to take advantage of as many marketing opportunities are we could. Using the five or more rule, each simple announcement was then repurposed into five more vehicles. These included a social media post, an internal/external newsletter article, a press release, a website banner, and a case study blog post.

Sometimes a seemingly small placement of a message can result in big exposure for a company if it is released at the epicenter of their audience. Every placement counts.

The Results

I learned that the old adage "with great success comes great responsibility" is absolutely true. We blew past our goal of $47,000, surpassing it by 116 percent to raise nearly $55,000 for the project. However, we now had to deliver in the creation of a 72,000-word book that would connect with the reader.

Over the next few months, *Top Fuel for Life* was ghostwritten in conjunction with Fig Factor Media, which I founded several years ago as a publishing and promotional vehicle for emerging authors. Our ghostwriter captured Jim O.'s voice in telling his inspirational story and, through intensive interviews and research, created the 262-page book that was published in 2015. We then set about promoting Jim O. not only as an author but as a speaker and media personality, setting up a website to engage him as a speaker and social media to begin building a book community.

Beginning with the official book launch, which took place at an NHRA race in Dallas, JJR propelled Jim O. into the media spotlight. We brought Jim's story to a myriad of media outlets, with an individual angle. Since Jim was already a semicelebrity on the racing circuit, the story of his experiences as an NHRA crew chief and friend of the Kalittas was well-received by industry media. Outlets included NHRA.com, Draglist.com, and *Hot Rod* and *Drag Illustrated* magazines, among many, many others. For lifestyle and general interest outlets, we pitched the inspirational story of one man's journey through life and learning the importance of family as he witnesses his wife's death from cancer and goes on to establish the Tammy O. Foundation. With this brand, Jim was invited for interviews with many local and national television and radio stations and also appeared in national media such as the *Detroit Free Press*.

To date, 72,000 copies of *Top Fuel* have been sold on Amazon.com with a 4.5 star rating. The book has also caught the attention and affirmation of celebrities such as Connie Kalitta, Alexa DiJoria, Jesse James, Chip Foose, and other well-known legendary crew chiefs from the National Hot Rod Association. Jim continues to tell his story on stage to audiences as well as in media interviews.

Work is often its own reward, but imagine how excited our team was to win the Silver Trumpet Award from the Publicity Club of Chicago for our efforts in Jim O.'s Kickstarter campaign. The Silver Trumpet is the most prestigious awards program for public relations professionals in the region and recognizes individual achievement in the planning, creativity, and execution of public relations and communications initiatives. The combination of JJR teamwork, the creation of *Top Fuel*, its consequent success on Amazon, and Jim O.'s ongoing media attention and fundraising for the Tammy O. Foundation make this one project I will never forget.

Part III: Advice for the Reader

As someone who has been in the field for a long time, there is a lot I would do differently if given the chance. To start, I would have embraced my authenticity sooner rather than wanting to be someone else. As a young woman and a person of color I was afraid to be different, but if I had started off as my authentic self it would have saved me many headaches. I wish I would have known that it was okay to be an energetic, passionate, and compassionate Latina full of ideas to achieve amazing success.

Trying to fit into an ecosystem, looking different than your coworkers, is very intimating. I had to learn to embrace myself and focus on my value to others without labeling myself. Once I accepted myself the way I was and brought the best of my culture into my life in the United States, I was surprised to realize that my differences could actually be an asset. In reviews from my clients now, I often hear how much people enjoy my perspective and the value that I bring, which is a result of my unique background. People connect with others who care, no matter what they look like or where they come from.

Because of my experiences, my best advice for people starting in PR is to be authentic, follow your passion, and help others. Personally, I believe a great way to stay organized and motivated is to journal about your goals, dreams, and wishes as well as your successes, and look back on it all when your career or your business get difficult. It will remind you of the "why" and get you back on track to produce magic for others.

As a final thought, people new to the field should continue to work to diversify their skills. I recommend studying various components of a typical marketing campaign such as social media, website management, search engine optimization, search engine marketing, market influencers, strategic alliances, out-of-home advertising, word of mouth, experiential marketing, and events. The more you know about how these vehicles work, the more ideas you will have to intelligently integrate them into public relations to produce results. At JJR, I created a deck of marketing cards as a guide for business to understand the correlation between cost and effectiveness of each one of these vehicles. You can download the free app here: http://www.marketingmix.mobi.

Jacqueline Camacho-Ruiz
CEO, JJR Marketing, Inc.
Facebook: facebook.com/JacquelineAuthor
Twitter: @JackieAmazing
Instagram: jacquelinecamachoruiz
websites: jackiecamacho.com, jjrmarketing.com, figfactormedia.com

12

PUBLIC RELATIONS RESOURCES

Kate S. Kurtin, Ph.D

The field of public relations is constantly changing and at a speed faster than any publisher can match. However, what does not change is history or the experience of entering and thriving in the field of public relations. What you read in *Public Relations in Practice* reflects the story of eleven people and their successful journeys in the field of PR. While each path was different, there were some key themes repeated and highlighted in the text.

Education

Many of our authors pursued an education in English, strategic communication, or mass communication. These fields teach valuable tools necessary for PR success. Further, following their undergraduate careers, many of the authors entered master's programs in fields related to public relations. While this is not necessary, it can be helpful. Master's programs in public relations or strategic communication combine education with experience. Most programs also feature top practitioners, mandatory internships, and work on skill-building in addition to pedagogy and theory. Furthermore, exposure from a master's program may lead to increased employment opportunities or may be useful in some businesses for promotion and leadership opportunities. That being said, PR is a creative industry, not necessarily an academic one. You must be good in order to survive, and you must have experience in order to get a job. Because of that, work experience and a solid portfolio are often of paramount importance. As you read, some of our authors found their experience and built their portfolio in school, while others worked their way up directly through work in the field.

Internships

As Christina writes in chapter 4, internships are often no longer optional to foster success in your early PR career. "Internships provide hands-on work experience and opportunities for students to build professional connections. According to monster.com, employers 'overwhelmingly point to an internship experience as the most important factor they consider in hiring new college grads for full-time positions'" (p. 45). There are many places to find internships in PR. The first is from a good Google search. If you search "internships in public relations" through Google, 468,000 results come up in 0.84 seconds. While these results may be overwhelming, and not particularly helpful, you can make good use of this search by focusing on the top results. For example, when I ran this search in August 2018, I found internship opportunities through www.glassdoor.com, www.indeed.com, www.CareerBliss.com, and www.internships.com. Of course, once you find an internship that looks interesting, you must do some background research. Find out as much about the company as you can before you even apply. You want to make sure that the opportunity is legitimate and that it is, in fact, what you are looking for. For example, compare the following two posts for internship positions:

First:

Forget making endless coffee runs, we expect our graduate interns to jump directly into client work, learning the ropes of what it takes to become a PR practitioner. From day one, our interns become integral parts of our team, many of whom get hired on as permanent employees. Opportunities are available across all areas of our business including:

- Consumer and lifestyle marketing
- Corporate reputation
- Sports marketing and sponsorship activation
- Technology (B2B and B2C)
- Healthcare qualifications

Our ideal candidates will have graduated and completed college coursework in journalism, public relations, communications or related fields. All of our graduate interns are expected to have:

- Excellent communications and critical thinking skills
- Excellent research, writing, and organization skills
- Extensive social media experience across multiple platforms
- An ability to work easily in both large team environments or independently
- An ability to multitask and thrive in a fast-paced environment
- A positive attitude and willingness to learn from our industry-leading team of counselors
- Prior internship experience at a public relations firm or corporate communications department. This is a full-time (40 hours per week), paid position for three months, with the opportunity to move into a full-time position at the completion of the program.

And, second:

This internship position is a key role in facilitating all aspects of PR. We have three departments, the PR showroom/celebrity team, media team, and rental showroom. In regards to assisting the showrooms, this will include doing pick-ups/drop-offs with merchandise, bagging up items, assisting stylists while in the showroom, merchandising and maintaining the aesthetics of the showrooms, and pitching up-and-coming and established designers to be represented. The media side works on blogger outreach and gifting, and ensuring any placements the celebrity team garnered are credited with designer information and secure placements of those shots in weekly/monthly magazines or online mentions, event planning/production. There will be the occasional opportunity to go on photo shoots and work events that are based in Los Angeles.

Expectations of an ideal candidate:

- Self-driven with a willingness to meet and exceed expectations
- Independent
- Can handle a fast pace environment
- Takes initiative, especially during slower periods
- Strong work ethic
- Burning desire to learn, serious ambition to be in the fashion industry
- GREAT attention to detail
- Sense of initiative, can work well with minimal direction
- Great decision-making skills
- Excellent written and oral communication skills
- Excels at research. Utilizing all resources to gather information
- Team spirit
- Upbeat, high energy level
- Positive, can-do attitude, go-getter
- Organized, able to think logically
- Able to take constructive criticism
- Creative problem-solver
- Reliable and punctual
- Has a strong interest in the world of public relations
- Having a car to run errands to celebs and celeb stylists
- Owns laptop to use during internship

This is an UNPAID academic or experience only internship. We are in need of hard working self-starters that can keep up with a fast-paced environment. Interns are expected to work 1–4 days a week (you choose your days) from the hours of 10:00 a.m. to 6:30 p.m. Monday–Friday. This is a two- or four-month commitment.

A credit of up to $500 (depending on length of internship) will be given to shop our rental showroom upon completion of internship.

Did you see the difference? The first opportunity will give you portfolio building, on-the-ground experience. The second one, while it sounds very exciting, may ultimately do little beyond put miles on your car and elevate you to gold card Starbucks status. Be critical when on these job sites.

Another option for finding internships through job websites is to go directly through a public relations firm. Most firms will list employment opportunities on their websites, and you can apply directly. While on their website, just as described above, you should review past clients, evaluate the type of work the firm does, and decide if that is what you can see yourself doing. Be self-reflective in this process. Do you want to work for Fortune 500 companies or local retailors? Or would you rather work for a nonprofit? Beyond this, ask yourself how you see yourself working: Would you rather work in-house and focus on one client, or do you want to work in a big agency and have many clients? Do you want to work with a large team and focus on one skill? Or a small team where you wear many hats? In order to correctly identify the best opportunities for your needs, you should have an idea of how each company operates before you apply. The majority of this information can be gathered from the company's website.

This internship advice remains valuable when you are on the job market. Be critical of the types of posts. Look for keywords and specifics about what the job entails. Be wary about any ambiguous terms like "marketing," as that typically means it is a position in sales working for a commission. Also, keep in mind the old adage that if it sounds too good to be true, it probably is. For instance, the second post above related to fashion sounds amazing: go on fashion shoots! Meet designers! But then it also states you must have a car and your own laptop— that's where the cracks show.

Of course, some important details will never appear in a job call or even an interview. For example, every one of our authors mentioned their mentor and how important it is to have one. Unfortunately, this is not generally the kind of information provided in the early stages of a job hunt. Instead, focus on trying to find a place where you can see yourself growing and thriving. Try to find a job where the company will value you and your experience more than your methods of transportation. As you can see from the chapters in this book, each of our career steps are connected, and the people you meet in your first internship and job will likely be the people who help you get your next job.

Relationships

On this point, the role and importance of relationships to careers in PR is changing. According to the Public Relations Society of America, "the earliest definitions of Public Relations emphasized press agentry and publicity, while more modern definitions incorporate the concepts of 'engagement' and 'relationship building.'"

As the authors in this book mentioned time and time again, relationships in PR are crucial. While each author emphasized different relationships, the concept of relationships with colleagues and mentors remained a consistent theme throughout. Nicole focused on the mentor–mentee relationship. In chapter 8, she explains, "A mentor is a person who will meet with you, who will give you strategic advice, and who will affirmatively go out of their way to help you. A mentor is a person who will give you honest feedback, even when it is negative. And don't mistake a friend, coworker, or supervisor for a mentor; that can seriously derail your journey.... If you can find that person, good for you. But keep looking and don't give up if you haven't yet found that person. And in the meantime, do your best to be that person to others. It is your professional duty" (p. 88). Alternatively, Devon focused on the relationship between PR agent and new reporters. In chapter 9, he writes, "Being a successful publicist requires that you build a network of reporters and editors and producers who trust you. If you can do this, then you leap ahead of thousands of publicists and have an easier time placing your story in the right place" (p. 96). This moves us into the next theme: What exactly is PR?

What PR Is, and What It Isn't

As Gineen writes in chapter 10, "PR is best described as a strategic process that requires patience, planning, and a purpose. It simply doesn't happen overnight" (p. 109). So often in movies and television shows PR is shown as all glitz and glam: Enter public relations and you will be famous! You will meet famous people, go on fashion shoots, and be best friends with celebrities! As I hope is clear from reading this book, PR can certainly be fast-paced, exciting, fun, and challenging, but very little of it is actually in the spotlight.

As Jillian explains in chapter 5, "Public relations is all about elevating another person, brand, business, or organization, and as a professional in this field, you tend to be behind the scenes. This behind-the-scenes work may come in the form of ghostwriting an article or crafting a quote for a press release, and is vital to the success of the campaign, but doesn't come with front-stage accolades. While everyone may not know that you were the actual author, the true gratitude comes from the success you are able to achieve for others, something especially gratifying in nonprofit PR" (p. 56). Similarly, Gineen shared that she was trying to become a radio personality when she found PR. "With entering into a career in public relations, I found that I had to rethink my dreams of being the talent. However, I have been pleasantly surprised to find it *more* rewarding to be behind the scenes" (p. 108).

Diversity

As you read in many of the chapters, inclusion and representation remains an issue in public relations. Gineen calls for us to be champions of diversity, and Jackie, in chapter 11, explains that her career catapulted once she embraced her diversity and accepted her "Latina within" (p. 116). Likewise, Arlene, in chapter 7, spoke about being the youngest member of her team, and one of a very small number of women. She explains that she "focused on establishing credibility by not getting caught up with office politics, making sound and well researched recommendations, identifying proof points to support recommendations, and, most importantly, forcing myself to ask for help when it was needed" (p. 73).

Echoing the sentiments of the chapters in this book, PR is about elevating a person, product, or brand. It is our express interest to do that for you as well. For that to happen, incorporate the lessons from this book into your own career, and the next edition could feature your story and your successes. Just know that when you are starting out you have no established credibility. Instead, rely on your education, research, and relationships to build your footing. Remember that there are millions of people who want the job that you have, and so you have to constantly be proving yourself. Ask questions, be mindful, and know that if you put in the time, it will pay off. I promise!

How to Be Successful

I would be remiss if I did not take an opportunity in my own chapter to highlight some of my professional tips. First, some things you can do:.

Read!

Become a voracious reader of media. Keep track of trends, follow influencers through social media, begin to recognize trends, and figure out what you are passionate about. Next, know who the best reporters are and start following them on social media as well. Do not shy away from positive social media engagement. If you can get agents and reporters to recognize your name, they will be much more interested in engaging back.

Get Professional Online

While you are following these influencers and reading everything in sight, make sure that your online profiles portray you as the professional you want to be. If necessary, start separate social media accounts that are professional and not personal. Create a Linked-In account and connect to professionals in the field and at firms you would like to work for. Do not be afraid to make professional contacts, because as we learned from the book, you never know where your next job will come from. Recall that Erik first answered phones for free, and Jackie was a hostess. It is vital that your early attempts at entering the field are positive and professional.

While reading and utilizing social media are the best things that you can do on your own to prepare yourself for a career in PR, there are also nationally recognized PR resources.

Public Relations Society of America (PRSA)

PRSA is a tremendous resource for every theme we have discussed. Indeed, in PRSA, PR is fortunate to have the nation's largest professional organization dedicated to preparing and connecting practitioners to resources throughout their career. PRSA offers its members opportunities in professional development and connects different PR disciplines in order to strengthen connections across the country. PRSA is committed to helping its members secure employment, maintain their positions, and enhance the field. With this mission, PRSA hosts "career-enhancing initiatives and programming including webinars; APR certification; awards; thought leadership; our members-only, exclusive private online community MyPRSA; resource library; publications; and conferences" (www.prsa.org/about/about-prsa). Through its website you can learn about PR, find job opportunities, find resources in your area, and even join a mentoring program.

Public Relations Student Society of America (PRSSA)

A spin-off of PRSA, PRSSA is an organization dedicated to students interested in public relations and communications (www.prssa.prsa.org). PRSSA operates by chapters, hosted by colleges and universities across the world. According to their website, PRSSA has "more than 10,000 students and advisers organized into 300 plus chapters in the United States, Argentina, Colombia and Peru." From its website you can see if there is a chapter at your local school. If there is a local PRSSA, once you join there are many membership benefits. First, PRSSA has resources for you to gain experience through internships, competitions, scholarships, and leadership opportunities. Furthermore, when you join PRSSA you join a network of over 10,000 peers and professionals. PRSSA can facilitate relationship building through conferences and events. Finally, PRSSA is a great resource to help you find a job. Not only does membership to PRSSA look good on your resume; being a part of PRSSA will give you valuable experience, and there is a PRSSA internship center where PR employment opportunities are posted and regularly updated.

International Association of Business Communicators (IABC)

The other side of public relations is strategic communication, and there is no better resource for strategic communicators than IABC. As it says on its website, IABC "is a global network of communication professionals committed to improving organizational effectiveness through strategic communication" (www. iabc.com). Similar to PRSA, IABC has professional resources, connections, and learning opportunities for PR practitioners. They host conferences and webinars, and a center for job opportunities. Unfortunately, they do not have a PRSSA equivalent.

Final Thoughts

I hope this book has been useful for you as you begin or continue your PR journey. It was our hope to expose you to parts of PR you may be unfamiliar with, show you how to think like a pro, and give you tangible advice for your own career. Know that for some of us the road is curved and may even contain hazards like law school and kids. For others that road may simply seem very steep starting at the bottom. Of course, there is no one way to succeed in public relations. Find what drives you and go all-in. Good luck in your career!

Kate S. Kurtin, Ph.D
Communication Studies Department
California State University, Los Angeles
LinkedIn: Kate Kurtin

CREDITS

Page 1, Photo 1.1 Karen Algeo Krizman; 4, Figure 1.1 Steve Krizman; 14, Photo 2.1
Owen Kolasinski; 19, Photo 3.1 Michael Ramirez; 31, Photo 4.1 Jim Gipe / Pivot
Media; 36, Figure 4.1 Courtesy of Forbes Library; 47, Photo 5.1 Ann Blanchard; 55,
Figure 5.1 The Cromwell Center for Disabilities and Awareness; 59, Photo 6.1 Strategic
Communications, LLC; 60, Figure 6.1 Pflanz Family; 65, Figure 6.2 Pflanz Family;
66, 6.3 Pflanz Family; 72, Photo 7.1 Steve Maller, MallerMedia; 80, Figure 7.1, Waking
State Design; 82, 7.2 Drew Altizer, https://drewaltizer.com; 85, Photo 8.1 Mary
Hennigan; 95, Photo 9.1 Zachary Story; 105, Photo 10.1 MasterMIND Productions /
Kenneth Branson; 114, Photo 11.1 Daisy Jimenez at DAI Brand; 122, Photo 12.1
California State University, Los Angeles.